PUT IT IN WRITING 1

Using Words

CAMBRIDGE Adult Education
Prentice Hall Regents, Englewood Cliffs, NJ 07632

Photo Credits

Page 2. *Top left:* Irene Springer. *Bottom left:* Marc P. Anderson. *Right:* Ken Karp.
Page 6. Ken Karp.
Page 18. The New York Convention & Visitors Bureau.
Page 27. Laimute E. Druskis.
Page 38. *Top left and Bottom:* Marc P. Anderson. *Top right:* United Press International, Inc.
Page 41. Marc P. Anderson.
Page 57. United Nations/Photo by B.P. Wolff.
Page 68. *Top:* WHO Photo by L. Almasi/K. Hemzo. *Middle:* Ken Karp. *Bottom:* Laimute E. Druskis.
Page 71. Marc P. Anderson.
Page 85. Eugene Gordon.
Page 98. *Top left:* Ken Karp. *Top right and Bottom:* Marc P. Anderson.
Page 101. Teri Leigh Stratford.

Cover and interior design by Caliber Design Planning Inc.

Written by Brian Schenk. Edited by Laura Daly.

Published by Prentice-Hall, Inc.
A Division of Simon & Schuster
Englewood Cliffs, New Jersey 07632

Printed in the United States of America

10 9 8 7 6 5 4 3

ISBN 0-8428-9717-8

Prentice-Hall International (UK) Limited, *London*
Prentice-Hall of Australia Pty. Limited, *Sydney*
Prentice-Hall Canada Inc., *Toronto*
Prentice-Hall Hispanoamericana, S.A., *Mexico*
Prentice-Hall of India Private Limited, *New Delhi*
Prentice-Hall of Japan, Inc., *Tokyo*
Simon & Schuster Asia Pte. Ltd., *Singapore*
Editora Prentice-Hall do Brasil, Ltda., *Rio de Janeiro*

Contents

Unit 1: Showing Time when You Write 3

Chapter 1: Writing about the Past, Present, and Future 6
Lesson 1: Showing Time in Your Sentences 7
Lesson 2: The Building Blocks of the System of Tenses 9
Lesson 3: Writing with the Present, Past, and Future Tenses 11

Chapter 2: Writing about Continuous Actions 19
Lesson 4: Using the Progressive Tenses 20
Lesson 5: Special Uses of the Present Progressive 23

Chapter 3: Writing with Other Kinds of Verb Helpers 28
Lesson 6: Using Helpers to Change the Meaning of a Verb 29
Lesson 7: Using Forms of Do to Help Verbs 32

Unit 1 Mastery Review 36

Unit 2: Writing Clear Sentences 39

Chapter 4: Writing Verbs to Agree with Subjects 41
Lesson 8: Checking Agreement with the It-versus-They Test 42
Lesson 9: Finding the Simple Subject to Check Agreement 45
Lesson 10: Checking Agreement with Compound Subjects 47
Lesson 11: Special Problems in Subject-and-Verb Agreement 50

Chapter 5: Writing with Pronouns 57
Lesson 12: Checking for Subjects and Direct Objects 58
Lesson 13: Checking for Indirect Objects 60
Lesson 14: Checking Pronouns Used with Prepositions 62

Unit 2 Mastery Review 65

Unit 3: Writing Descriptive Sentences 70

Chapter 6: Descriptive Writing with Adjectives and Adverbs 71
Lesson 15: Telling the Difference between Adjectives and Adverbs 73
Lesson 16: Using Linking Verbs and Adjectives 78
Lesson 17: Making Adjectives and Adverbs Stronger 80

Chapter 7: Putting Adjectives and Adverbs in the Right Place 85
Lesson 18: Adding Adjectives 87
Lesson 19: Adding Adverbs 89

Unit 3 Mastery Review 96

Unit 4: Showing Special Relationships 99

Chapter 8: Writing about the Past and Future—Special Cases 101
Lesson 20: Present Perfect Tense 103
Lesson 21: Past Perfect Tense 107
Lesson 22: Future Perfect Tense 111

Unit 4 Mastery Review 121

Final Mastery Test 123

Answer Key 129

To the User

Here's how to use this book to improve your writing:

- TRY IT OUT. You will do these to practice the basics of written English. These are not tests; they are learning activities.
- IN YOUR OWN WORDS. These ask you to write your own complete sentences, not merely to correct or finish sentences you've been given.
- CHECK YOUR SKILLS. These will help you find out how well you remember the structures you have studied.
- PUT IT IN WRITING. These give you a chance to put to work all the skills you've mastered in a chapter, a unit, or the whole book.
- UNIT MASTERY REVIEW. At the end of each unit, you get to SHOW WHAT YOU KNOW about the grammar lessons in the unit and to use your skills in a PUT IT IN WRITING assignment.
- FINAL MASTERY TEST. After taking this test, you will be able to decide whether you need to review any of the lessons in this book.
- AN EDITING GUIDE on the inside covers of this book will help you capitalize and punctuate correctly in the sentences you write.

Using the Activity Book for Practice in Real-Life Writing

PUT IT IN WRITING 1	ACTIVITY BOOK 1
Unit 1: Narration	**Unit 1:** Applying Narration in Letters • Using Verbs
Unit 2: Persuasion	**Unit 2:** Applying Persuasion in Letters • Using Agreement Pronouns
Unit 3: Description	**Unit 3:** Applying Description in Letters • Using Adjectives and Adverbs
Unit 4: Informative Writing	**Unit 4:** Applying Informative Writing in Letters • Using Perfect Tenses

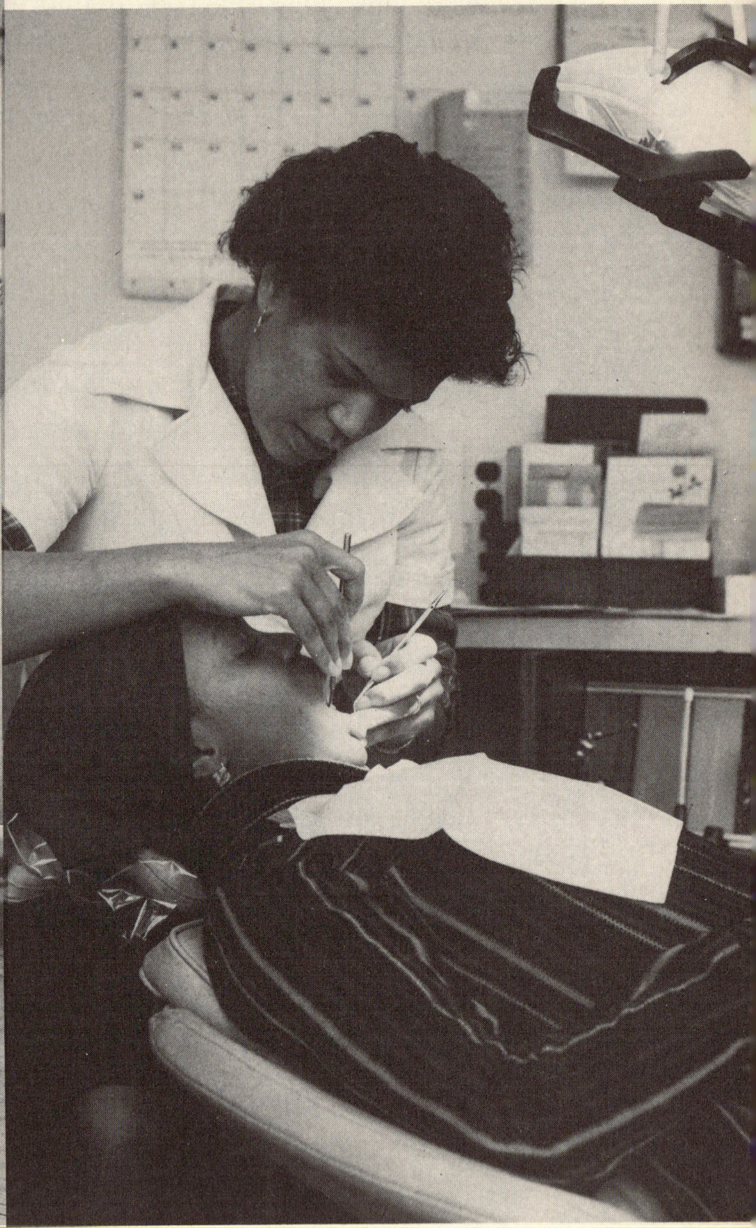

UNIT 1

Showing Time when You Write

Words don't exist for themselves. They have a purpose. They are used to express ideas and opinions. They can be used to tell what happened. Words can be used to say who you are and what you know and believe.

When you write, you have a purpose, a reason for writing. Knowing your purpose before you start writing can help you present your ideas and thoughts more clearly. One purpose for writing is to tell a story. You could tell what happened at a baseball game last week. You could say what you plan to do today. Or you could list the things you would do if you won the state lottery. This type of writing is called **narrative.**

Historical writing is narrative. It is a record of what actually happened, or it is an effort to re-create what happened. You could tell the events in a person's life; this is called writing a biography. Or you could give the main incidents in a country's past, its history. You could even tell about events in your own life; this would be writing your autobiography. A letter can also be a form of narrative.

News writing is narrative. It, too, is a record of what happened. You could tell what happened in a car accident. Or you can say what your city is doing to cope with a water shortage, perhaps.

Story writing is also narrative. A story is about make-believe characters and events. It can explore a single event, or it can show events taking place over a long period of time. Historical writing and news writing tell us: These are the facts about what happened. Story writing says: If these were the facts, this would have happened.

In order to tell about something, you have to write your sentences in time. You need to say what happened (in the past), what is happening right now (in the present), or what is going to happen (in the future). This Unit will help you learn how to use verb forms to express time in your writing. You will practice writing verbs as you begin to write narratives.

Before You Begin

Put an X in the box next to the answer that best completes the sentence.

If you're writing a narrative, you are mainly trying

☐ a. to convince your reader that your opinion is the one that's correct.

☐ b. to make the scene you describe seem "real" for your reader.

☐ c. to tell a story in a clear and lively way for your reader.

☐ d. to explain to the reader how to get a job done.

If you put an X in the box next to c, you understand the most important point in writing a narrative. A narrative is a story. And your job as a writer of narratives is to make your stories clear and interesting for your reader.

Brainstorming

Take another look at the photos that started this Unit. Each photo could be a picture that illustrates a narrative.

In the spaces below, write at least one word for each photo. Each word should be one that could be used in telling the story in the photo. The word could be the name of something shown in the photo. Or it could be a word that describes an action in the photo. You can even give words that tell the changing moods of the people in the photo: first, how they felt before the photo was shot; next, how they felt while they were being photographed; last, how they felt after the photographer said, "Okay, relax!"

After that, choose one more word that could be used in writing a narrative. This time, choose a word that could be used in telling a story from your own life. It could be the name of something you made or did or had. Or it could be somewhere you went, or someone you knew. Or it could be a word that describes the way you did something special.

You'll use these "key words" later, at the end of this Unit, after you've mastered the lessons in Chapters 1 through 4.

Photo 1: ______________________________

Photo 2: ______________________________

Photo 3: ______________________________

My Own Life: ______________________________

CHAPTER 1

Writing about the Past, Present, and Future

Think about the people in this photo. What were they doing before they got together? What is happening now in the photo? What will happen after the song is over?

When you write a narrative, you know what time period you are writing about. You know whether you are telling about something that has already happened or something that is happening right now or something that hasn't happened yet. Your job as a writer is to make this clear to your readers.

In this chapter, we will review the three main tenses of verbs, to help you use the right word to make your sentences clear about the past, the present, and the future.

LESSON 1: Showing Time in Your Sentences

Remember, a **verb** is usually a word that names an action. A verb tells what someone or something did, or is doing, or is going to do sometime. A verb can also tell what someone or something was, or always is, or is right now, or is going to be in the future. The word that the verb tells about is called the **subject** of the verb. For example:

I	see	you.
subject	**verb**	

You	see	me.
subject	**verb**	

In the first sentence, I am the one who is doing the seeing. So "I" is the subject of the sentence. In the second sentence, you are the one who is doing the seeing. So "you" is the subject of the second sentence. You know that every verb has a subject. And every sentence has a verb. So every sentence is about doing or being in the past, present, or future.

If you write your verbs carefully, you will clearly tell your readers what point in time you are writing about. Think of time as a road that runs from what happened in the past to what is happening right now to what is going to happen in the future. This can be pictured as a straight line. Everything that happens takes place at some point on the line of time:

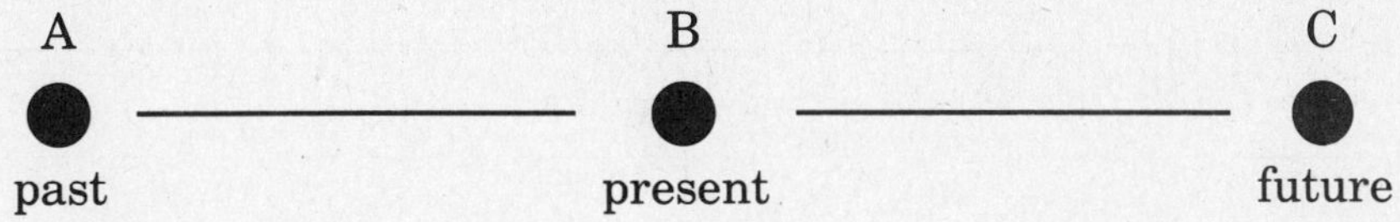

Try It Out

Here are six sentences about the action of writing. We have underlined the verbs. By changing the form of the verb, we have moved the action to a different point on the time line. At what point on the line would you put each of these sentences? Write the letter of that point in the blank space next to each sentence:

1. I <u>write</u> something every day. ____
2. I <u>am writing</u> something now. ____
3. I <u>wrote</u> something yesterday. ____
4. I <u>have written</u> you letters before. ____
5. I <u>will write</u> something tomorrow. ____
6. I <u>am going to write</u> letters tomorrow. ____

Sentences 1 and 2 are about something that is true at the present moment in time, which is point **B** on our line. Sentences 3 and 4 are about something that happened in the past, which is point **A** on our line. And sentences 5 and 6 are about something that will happen in the future, which is point **C** on our line.

In Your Own Words

Try writing three sentences about yourself. The first one should be about your past. Tell about something you once did or used to do, or something you once were or used to be—but make it something you no longer do or no longer are.

Your second sentence should be about the present. Tell about something you are doing right now or something you do from time to time.

Your third sentence should be about your future. Tell about something that you know will happen to you, or tell about something you expect to happen to you, either soon or a long time from now.

1. I ______________________________
2. I ______________________________
3. I ______________________________

Compare your sentences with those on page 129.

LESSON 2: The Building Blocks of the System of Tenses

As you can see, verbs give important information to readers. In our examples in TRY IT OUT on page 8, we added words such as now, yesterday, and tomorrow to make the time more clear. But the verbs all by themselves can tell a reader when the action in a sentence happens. For example, the verbs in the following two sentences tell you that they are not about the same point in time.

I wrote a letter.

I will write a letter.

The different forms of verbs that tell about time are called **verb tenses.** In our examples, we used six different verb tenses. The word tense simply means a group of verb forms that are put together in the same basic way and that describe the same idea about time. It can take time and hard work to become a master at using the English verb tenses, but it's worth it. Your writing will be much clearer if you choose your verb tenses on purpose and not by accident.

All possible verb tenses use one of four basic forms of the main verb. These forms are called the **principal parts** of the verb.

Simple Form	**Simple Past Form**	**Past Participle (have +)**	**Present Participle (be +)**	
talk	talked	talked	talking	*regular*
hurry	hurried	hurried	hurrying	
plan	planned	planned	planning	
decide	decided	decided	deciding	
bring	brought	brought	bringing	*irregular*
write	wrote	written	writing	
break	broke	broken	breaking	
know	knew	known	knowing	
give	gave	given	giving	
forget	forgot	forgotten	forgetting	
buy	bought	bought	buying	
spend	spent	spent	spending	
hurt	hurt	hurt	hurting	
am, is, are	was, were	been	being	
have, has	had	had	having	

The first three verbs in this chart are called **regular verbs.** They are called regular because the past form and the past participle are always formed by adding -d or -ed to the end of the simple form. Most verbs in English are regular verbs. The only problem you may have with these verbs is a spelling problem. For most verbs that end with an e, you must remember to drop the final e before adding -ed or -ing. Other spelling changes can be difficult to remember. Do you change a final y to an i before adding -ed? Do you double a final consonant before adding -ed or -ing? The spelling tips on the inside covers of this book should help you solve many of these problems.

The other verbs in our chart of principal parts are **irregular verbs.** Until you have memorized the forms of the irregular verbs, use a dictionary for help. In the dictionary, after the simple form of the verb, you will find a listing of all irregular forms. We'll give you practice using irregular verbs. Keep a notebook of any verbs that give you trouble. Study these verbs and memorize their irregular forms.

The last two irregular verbs in the chart are be and have. These two verbs can be used alone. But they can be used in another important way, too. They can be used together with another verb to form different verb tenses. When they are used in this way, we call the verb that names the action the **main verb.** The verbs be and have are then **helping verbs.** They help the main verb show a particular time. You will be using the verb be as a helping verb in the three tenses we'll talk about in Chapter 2 in this unit. You will be using the verb have as a helping verb in the tenses we'll talk about in Unit 4. Because these two verbs are used so often, make sure you know their irregular forms.

Try It Out

Fill in the blanks. Make any necessary spelling changes when you add -ed or -ing to a verb.

1. apply + ed = ____________	2. carry + ed = ____________
3. dry + ed = ____________	4. obey + ed = ____________
5. destroy + ed = ____________	6. deny + ed = ____________
7. argue + ing = ____________	8. date + ing = ____________
9. choose + ing = ____________	10. smoke + ing = ____________
11. lie + ing = ____________	12. tie + ing = ____________
13. beg + ed = ____________	14. fan + ing = ____________

15.	drop	+ ed	=	____________	16.	fix	+ ing	=	____________
17.	slip	+ ed	=	____________	18.	train	+ ing	=	____________
19.	prefer	+ ing	=	____________	20.	occur	+ ed	=	____________

Check your answers on page 129.

In Your Own Words

Look at the verbs in this story. Underline the verbs that are misspelled or used incorrectly. Then complete this narrative with your own version of what happened. Watch your verb tenses.

[1]This morning I learned that my pickup was broke. [2]I was planning to get a new starter, but I forgot. [3]I had no way to get to work. [4]I decideed to walk. [5]My brother had gave me a Walkman for Christmas. [6]So I brung it with me. [7]I listened to music as I hurryed along.

[8]____.

[9]____.

Check your answers on page 129.

LESSON 3: Writing with the Present, Past, and Future Tenses

On our time line on page 7, we showed you the three general points in time you might want to write about. The three tenses shown in the following chart help you tell a reader which of these three points you mean. These tenses give very simple information. They tell only whether an action is in the present, the past, or the future.

Today	Yesterday	Tomorrow
Present	*Past*	*Future*
I speak	I spoke	I will speak
he speaks	he spoke	he will speak
they speak	they spoke	they will speak

Did you notice that we added an -s to the present-tense verb when the subject was he? This is an important rule to remember about the present tense. Whenever the subject is he, she, or it—or a word that could be replaced by he, she, or it—add an -s or -es to the simple form in the present tense.

Now let's take a close look at the meanings of these basic verb tenses. Along the way, we'll ask you to try using the tenses in a few sentences.

A. Present Tense

This tense is for facts of life that are always true. It can also tell the reader that the writer knows that something is true at the present moment. That truth may be a statement about a habit that someone has now.

> Power tends to corrupt. Absolute power corrupts absolutely.
> Because my guitar is broken, it sounds terrible.
> They play basketball every day at school.

Try It Out

Fill in the blanks in the sentences below with the present tense of the verbs given in parentheses.

1. The sun ____________________ in the east. **(rise)**
2. I ____________________ to work every day. **(walk)**
3. My husband never ____________________ coffee. **(drink)**

You can use the verb form rises in sentence 1. The sentence tells about a fact that is always true. You can use the verb form walk in sentence 2 and the verb form drinks in sentence 3. These sentences then tell about a habit that someone has now.

The present tense may also be used to state a fact about an action that will take place in the future.

> My mother's plane arrives at ten o'clock tonight.

The plane will arrive at a specific time in the future. But this is a fact the writer knows now. So the present tense can be used.

In Your Own Words

Write three sentences of your own using the present tense.

1. Write about a habit someone you know has now.

____

2. Tell us a fact that is always true.

____

3. Tell us a fact about something that will happen later today.

____

Compare your sentences with those on page 129.

B. Past Tense

This tense shows that the action began and ended in the past. It tells about something that was true in the past.

> When I was six years old, my family moved to Atlanta.
>
> We bought a used car last night.
>
> Confucius was an ancient Chinese philosopher.

Try It Out

Fill in the blanks in the sentences below with the past tense of verbs given in parentheses.

1. I ____________________ a new job yesterday. **(start)**
2. The waiter ____________________ our order an hour ago. **(take)**
3. Martin Luther King, Jr., ____________________ the Nobel Peace Prize in 1964. **(receive)**

You can use the verb forms started in sentence 1 and took in sentence 2. These sentences then tell about actions that began and ended in the past. You can use the verb form received in sentence 3 to tell about something that was true in the past.

In Your Own Words

Write three sentences of your own using the past tense.

1. Tell about something you did yesterday.

   ____

2. Tell something you did as a child.

   ____

3. Tell the first thing you did when you got up today.

   ____

Compare your sentences with those on page 129.

C. Future Tenses

There are several ways to write about the future. You've seen that the present tense can describe a fact about the future. Here are three more ways to show future action:

will + main verb

I will think about that tomorrow.

She will call you later.

The helping word will tells the reader that the action will happen at some point in the future.

am, is, or are + going to + main verb

I am going to make dinner tonight.

She is going to take the day off tomorrow.

You are going to win next week's election.

The helping words am, is, or are plus going to are often used to say that the future action is part of a plan. These words can also show a prediction.

am, is, or are + about to + main verb

I am about to leave now.

The president is about to give a speech.

You are about to trip on that wire.

The helping words am, is, or are plus about to tell you that the future action is very close at hand.

Try It Out

Use the three different ways to show future action.

1. My parents ______________________________ their fiftieth wedding anniversary. **(celebrate)**
2. He ______________________________ the winner of the mayoral election. **(announce)**
3. Georgetown ______________________________ on network television. **(play)**

You can use the verb form are going to celebrate in sentence 1. This sentence tells about something that will definitely happen in the future. You can use the verb form is about to announce in sentence 2. This sentence tells about something that will happen very soon. You can use the verb form will play in sentence 3. This sentence that tells about something that will happen, but the date doesn't have to be definite, and it doesn't have to happen very soon. It may happen several times in the future, even over and over again.

In Your Own Words

Write three sentences of your own showing future action.

1. Tell about something you will do tomorrow.

   ____

2. Tell about something someone you know plans to do.

   ____

3. Tell what is going to happen to several people very soon.

   ____

Compare your sentences with those on page 130.

Check Your Skills: Write about Actions in the Past, Present, and Future

Use the past tense to complete the following sentences.

1. I ______________________ you a letter yesterday. **(write)**
2. The President of the United States ______________________ before the General Assembly at the United Nations. **(speak)**
3. Because of the extreme cold, one of the water pipes ____________ last night. **(burst)**
4. Last year, we ______________________ our own tomatoes. **(grow)**
5. The hurricane last Friday ______________________ down many trees. **(blow)**
6. Hernandez ______________________ the final out in last night's game. **(catch)**
7. Bees ______________________ a nest in our garage. **(build)**
8. Adam ______________________ me ten dollars recently. **(bet)**
9. My son ______________________ home at two o'clock this morning. **(come)**
10. The visitors ______________________ the local team for the championship. **(beat)**

Use the present tense to complete the following sentences.

11. Water ______________________ at 212° Fahrenheit. **(boil)**
12. Marty ______________________ shoes for a living. **(sell)**
13. His opinion ______________________ weight in the office. **(carry)**
14. My wife ______________________ English at night. **(teach)**
15. Mother Teresa ______________________ to comfort the sick and dying. **(try)**

Use <u>am</u>, <u>is</u>, or <u>are</u> plus <u>going to</u> to make the following sentences show a future action.

16. I ______________________ the doctor tomorrow. **(see)**

17. He ______________________ his job next Friday. **(quit)**

18. You ______________________ your date tonight. **(like)**

Use am, is, or are plus about to to make the following sentences show a future action.

19. Don't leave now. Sarah ______________________. **(sing)**

20. I just know you ______________________ something stupid. **(say)**

Check your answers on page 130.

Check Your Skills: Change the Time of Actions in a Paragraph

Read the following narrative paragraph. Each sentence is about something that will happen in the future. Rewrite the paragraph to make it about the past.

Then write at least two more sentences of your own to tell what happened next.

Tomorrow, I will go to the store. I am going to buy things for your birthday. While I am there, I will get a new tube of toothpaste. I will also choose a tube of fancy icing for your cake.

Lask week, ____

____

____

____

____

____

Check your answers on page 130.

Put It in Writing

Pretend that you are the guitar player in the photo at the start of this chapter. Write at least three sentences. They are for a letter you would send to one of the children in the photo. Tell about the day that you all sang together.

Write your first sentence in the past, starting with We were. Write your second sentence in the present, starting with We are. Write your third sentence in the future, starting with We will. Then continue your letter, if you wish.

We were ____

____

We are ____

____

We will ____

____

____

____

____

____

CHAPTER 2

Writing about Continuous Actions

Think about the activities shown in this photo. What is happening in the photo now that is very much like what happened here yesterday and the day before that, too? What is happening that is likely to be pretty much the same tomorrow?

Many actions you write about do not happen at a single point in the past, present, or future. Sometimes, the actions you describe take place over a period of time. For example, right now (in the present), you are reading this book. You started at some point before now (the past), and you are continuing to read (for a time into the future).

Three special tenses, the progressive tenses, help you show actions taking place over a period of time.

LESSON 4: Using the Progressive Tenses

You show the continuing nature of the action with the present participle (-ing form) of the main verb. You show the time period with a form of be:

Present Progressive	Past Progressive	Future Progressive
I am speaking	I was speaking	I will be speaking
She is speaking	She was speaking	She will be speaking
They are speaking	They were speaking	They will be speaking

A. The Present Progressive

The present tense of be (am, is, or are) plus the -ing form of the main verb shows that the action is taking place now:

I am listening to you.
He is eating lunch.
They are playing cards.

In all of these sentences, the action started at some point in the past. It is continuing to happen right now in the present.

Try It Out

Do you know the correct forms of be to use? Check your knowledge by filling in the blanks in these sentences with the correct present-tense form.

1. I ____________ thinking about you.

2. You ____________ breaking my heart.

3. She ____________ wearing a new sweater.

4. They ____________ saving a seat for you.

The correct answers are am, are, is, and are. Use am with the subject I. Use is with the subjects he, she, and it—or subjects that can be replaced by he, she, and it. For all other subjects, use are.

In Your Own Words

Write three sentences of your own using the present progressive tense. Use am, is, or are with the present participle (-ing form) of a verb.

1. Tell what you are doing right now.

   ____

2. Tell what one person around you is doing right now.

   ____

3. Tell what several people around you are doing right now.

   ____

Compare your sentences with those on page 130.

B. The Past Progressive

The past tense of be (was or were) plus the -ing form of the main verb shows that the action took place in the past:

> I was eating dinner when you called.
> The dog was making too much noise, so I let him out.
> You were talking in your sleep again last night.

In all of these sentences, the action lasted for some time in the past. It took more time than a single moment. The action was happening in the past, and it ended some time before the present.

Try It Out

Do you know which subjects take was and which subjects take were? Place an X in the box next to the subjects that take was:

☐ I ☐ you ☐ he or she ☐ it ☐ we
☐ they ☐ subjects that can be replaced by he, she, or it

You use was with the subjects I, he, she, or it—and subjects that can be replaced by he, she, or it. For all other subjects, you use were.

In Your Own Words

Write three sentences of your own using the past progressive tense. Use was or were with the present participle (-ing form) of a verb.

1. Tell something you did for several hours yesterday.

   ____

2. Tell what one person you know did for several hours yesterday.

   ____

3. Tell what a group of people you know did for several hours yesterday.

   ____

Compare your sentences with those on page 130.

C. The Future Progressive

The future tense of be (will be) plus the -ing form of the main verb shows that the action will take place in the future:

I will be sleeping by the time you call.
He will be working every night next week.
You will be freezing if you wear that coat.

In all of these sentences, the action will last for some time in the future. It has not yet started. But, when it does start, it will last for more than a moment.

Try It Out

Practice using the future progressive tense, using the verbs in parentheses.

1. I ____________________ for you at the bus station. **(wait)**
2. We ____________________ to the store later. **(go)**
3. The factory ____________________ next month. **(close)**

You could use will be waiting in sentence 1, will be going in sentence 2, and will be closing in sentence 3.

In Your Own Words

Write three sentences of your own using the future progressive tense. Use will be with the present participle (-ing form) of a verb.

1. Tell what you will be doing for several hours tomorrow.

____

2. Tell what someone else will be doing for several hours tomorrow.

____

3. Tell what a group of people will be doing for several hours tomorrow.

____

Compare your sentences with those on page 130.

LESSON 5: Special Uses of the Present Progressive

Like the simple present tense, the present progressive tense can be used to talk about habits. But compare the slight difference in meaning:

Simple Present	Present Progressive
1. He smokes too much.	He is smoking too much.
2. She always talks about you.	She is always talking about you.

Try It Out

The simple present tense makes a simple statement of fact. What difference in meaning do you get with the change to present progressive? Put an X in the box next to the correct answer:

1. In the first sentence, the present progressive tense emphasizes that:
   - ☐ a. his smoking is a habit that is going on now.
   - ☐ b. this is a fact of life that is always true.
2. In the second sentence, the present progressive tense emphasizes:
   - ☐ a. the continuous nature of her talking.
   - ☐ b. this is an action that is going on right now.

Remember that the progressive tenses show actions that take place over a period of time. So in the first sentence, this tense emphasizes that the person's smoking habit is going on now. In the second sentence, it emphasizes the continuous nature of her talking.

The present progressive tense can also be used to describe actions that will take place in the future

I am working late tomorrow.
I will be working late tomorrow.

He is leaving next week.
He will be leaving next week.

We are moving this coming Saturday.
We will be moving this coming Saturday.

In Your Own Words

Try using the present progressive to show future actions. Fill in the blanks in the following sentences with any verb you like. Just make sure it is in the present progressive tense. You can also add any other words you may need to make a complete sentence.

1. My best friend ______________________________ next weekend.
2. We ______________________________ tonight.
3. I ______________________________ tomorrow.

Compare your sentences with those on page 131.

Check Your Skills: Write about Actions with Progressive Tenses

Use the **present progressive tense** to complete the following sentences. Use the correct form of be with the -ing form of the verb given in parentheses at the end of each sentence.

1. I ______________________ this game. **(win)**
2. He ______________________ his mind. **(lose)**
3. We ______________________ verb tenses tomorrow. **(study)**
4. She ______________________ always ______________________ about her job. **(complain)**
5. They ______________________ about giving me a raise. **(think)**

Use the **past progressive tense** to complete the following sentences. Use the correct form of be with the -ing form of the verb given at the end of each sentence.

6. I ______________________ a shower when the phone rang. **(take)**
7. They ______________________ until two o'clock this morning. **(sing)**
8. The spy ______________________ to kill the President, but the FBI caught him. **(plan)**
9. You ______________________ boring, so I left. **(become)**
10. My friends ______________________ for you everywhere last night. **(look)**

Use the **future progressive tense** to complete the following sentences. Use the correct form of be with the -ing form of the verb given in parentheses at the end of the sentence.

11. Don't call me after 10:00. I ______________________ . **(sleep)**
12. I'm sure he won't be asleep at this hour. Probably he ______________ ______________ television. **(watch)**
13. We ______________________ for your call. **(wait)**

14. They ________________________ us soon. **(see)**

15. For the rest of the day, this station ________________________ emergency weather information. **(transmit)**

Check your answers on page 131.

Check Your Skills: Change the Time Shown by the Verbs in a Paragraph

Read the following paragraph. It uses the simple present tense to talk about facts that are true now. Rewrite the paragraph to show that the paragraph is about actions that are going on over a period of time. We have rewritten the first sentence for you.

Then write at least two more sentences of your own. Give other examples of change that you know about.

> In our company, things do change. Workers today get better pay and work fewer hours than before. Bosses take their workers' advice for improvements. The company gives free day care for employees' children. It even holds free exercise classes every day at noon.

In our company, things are changing. ________________________

____

____

____

____

____

____

____

____

____

Check your answers on page 131.

Put It in Writing

Pretend you are telling stories. Complete the following sentences in each narrative with the tenses given in parentheses. You may want to use the photo at the start of this chapter for ideas.

Story 1

1. One day last week, I ____________________

____________________. **(past progressive)**

2. I ____________________

____________________. **(past tense)**

3. Suddenly, ____________________

____________________. **(past progressive)**

Story 2

4. Let me tell you about a dream I often have. In it I ____________________

____________________. **(present progressive)**

5. I ____________________

____________________. **(present progressive)**

6. Suddenly, ____________________

____________________ **(present)**, and

7. I ____________________

____________________. **(present progressive)**

Story 3

8. In the year 2020 I will be ____________________ years old.

I ____________________. **(future progressive)**

9. People ____________________. **(future progressive)**

CHAPTER 3

Writing with Other Kinds of Verb Helpers

Think about the accident shown in this photo. What must have happened before the photo was shot? What may be happening now? What could happen in the next few minutes? What should happen soon, if everyone knows what to do?

In the tenses we have looked at so far, we have used the verb be to help verbs show different meanings. We have also used will, be going to, and be about to to help verbs show future time. In this chapter, we'll show you how to use some other kinds of helping verbs.

LESSON 6: Using Helpers to Change the Meaning of a Verb

The following helpers can give many different meanings to a verb.

can	might	would	need to
could	ought to	must	want to
may	should	used to	have to

Try It Out

What happens to the idea of a fact when we add a helper to the simple form of a verb? Put an X in the box next to the correct explanations of the following sentences:

1. I ought to get more sleep.
   This is something that the writer thinks
   ☐ a. should be a fact ☐ b. is a possible fact
2. She could hurt herself.
   This is something that the writer thinks
   ☐ a. should be a fact ☐ b. is a possible fact
3. He might want a divorce.
   This is something that the writer thinks
   ☐ a. should be a fact ☐ b. is a possible fact

In sentence 1, the helping words ought to let you know that the writer thinks the statement should be a fact. In sentences 2 and 3, could and might tell you that these are possibly facts.

When you use the present-tense form with one of the helpers in our list, you never add an -s or -es to the verb.

He takes taxis to work.	She wears my sweaters.
He could take a bus.	She can wear my sweaters.

These helpers can be used with the present participle (-ing form) when the verb be is also added.

Try It Out

Put an X in the box next to the correct explanations of the following sentences.

1. He must be sleeping late. He isn't here yet. The writer is talking about
   - ☐ a. something that is probably happening now.
   - ☐ b. something that is probably a habit.
   - ☐ c. a fact about an action that will take place over a period of time or in the future.
2. You should be taking more vitamins. The writer is talking about
   - ☐ a. something that is probably happening now.
   - ☐ b. something that would be a good habit.
   - ☐ c. something that should be a fact about an action that will take place over a period of time or in the future.
3. We may be seeing her tomorrow. The writer is talking about
   - ☐ a. something that is possibly happening now.
   - ☐ b. something that is possibly a habit.
   - ☐ c. something that is possibly a fact about an action that will take place over a period of time or in the future.

The correct answers are a, b, and c. The -ing form of the verb gave the sentences the meanings that the present progressive tense can give. In sentence 1, it told you that the writer was talking about a continuous action in the present. In sentence 2, it told you that the writer was talking about a person's habits. And in sentence 3, it told you that the writer was talking about a fact the writer knows about the future. The words must, should, and may gave you the additional information you found in your answers to our questions.

Most of these helpers never change form. However, you must show an appropriate verb form with the helpers need to, want to, or have to.

Try It Out

Write the numbers of the sentences that are about the present in the blank after "Sentences about the present." Write the numbers of the sentences that are about the past in the blank after "Sentences about the past." Write the numbers of the sentences that are about the future in the blank after "Sentences about the future."

1. They need to work harder.
2. They needed to work harder.
3. They will need to work harder.

4. They want to go.
5. They wanted to go.
6. They will want to go.
7. They have to think about it.
8. He has to think about it.
9. They had to think about it.
10. They will have to think about it.

Sentences about the present: ____________________

Sentences about the past: ____________________

Sentences about the future: ____________________

Sentences 1, 4, 7, and 8 are about the present. This is shown by using the present-tense forms need, want, have, and has. Sentences 2, 5, and 9 are about the past. This is shown by using the past-tense forms needed, wanted, and had. Sentences 3, 6, and 10 are about the future. This is shown by using the future-tense forms will need, will want, and will have.

In Your Own Words

Write three sentences of your own using any of the helpers from the list on page 29.

1. Tell something you think all people should do to get more out of life.

____

____

2. Tell what someone you know might be doing right now.

____

____

3. Tell something you wanted to do yesterday.

____

____

Compare your sentences with those on page 131.

LESSON 7: Using Forms of Do to Help Verbs

The words do, does, did, don't, doesn't, and didn't also help verbs. They can add special emphasis or show surprise as in the following examples.

Try It Out

Place an X in the blank under the column that describes what meaning these words add:

	Emphasis	Surprise
1. You hate my cooking. No, we do like your cooking.	☐	☐
2. I knew it all the time. She does love me.	☐	☐
3. I don't believe it! You did forget my birthday.	☐	☐

In examples 1 and 2, the words do and does add emphasis. In the first, do stresses just how untrue it is to say that the writer hates the cooking. In the second, the writer stresses that not only does she love him, she really loves him. The present-tense forms do and does emphasize that these statements are true right now. In the last example, the word did shows surprise. The writer is shocked that the person actually forgot. The past-tense form did is used because the action of forgetting began and ended in the past.

These words also help you make questions or negative statements out of a present- or past-tense sentence.

Try It Out

Fill in the blanks in the following chart. In the "Question" column, turn the statement into a question. In the "Negative" column, make the statement negative.

Statement	Question	Negative
1. He loves her.	______ he love her?	He ______ love her.
2. They work here.	______ they work here?	They ______ work here.
3. Someone saw you.	______ someone ______ you?	They ______ me.

You must use does and doesn't with the subjects he, she, or it—or subjects that can be replaced by he, she, or it. So, for the first sentence, you had to write: "Does he love her?" and "He doesn't love her."

All other subjects must use do and don't. So, for the second sentence, you had to write: "Do they work here?" and "They don't work here."

The words did and didn't already show past action. You don't use the past form of the main verb when you use these words. So, for the third sentence, you had to write: "Did someone see you?" and "They didn't see me."

In Your Own Words

Write sentences of your own. Follow the directions in front of the blanks.

1. Use do, does, or did for emphasis.

____

2. Ask a question about a fact.

____

3. Ask a question about a person's habit.

____

4. Answer the question you asked in sentence 3. Say, "No."

____

Compare your sentences with those on page 131.

Check Your Skills: Use Verb Helpers

Rewrite each of the following sentences. Use the helper given in parentheses at the end of each sentence to change the meaning. The first one has been done as an example.

1. She watches that show every Friday. **(used to)**

   She used to watch that show every Friday.

2. He is working. **(should)**

   ____

3. That coat costs a fortune. (**must**)

4. They are eating dinner. (**may**)

5. She understands your reasons. (**would**)

Check your answers on page 131.

Check Your Skills: Use Forms of Do

Rewrite the following sentences. Add do, does, or did to add emphasis or show surprise.

1. He looks better without his beard.

2. I want to go to the party.

3. That rabbit's foot brought me good luck.

4. You want to marry me!

Rewrite the following sentences. Turn them into questions.

5. He drinks coffee.

6. Her parents understood her decision.

7. Your doctor gives you sleeping pills.

Rewrite the following sentences. Make them negative.

8. He takes things very seriously.

____

9. They knew the answer.

____

10. My mother wants to live in the nursing home.

____

Check your answers on pages 131–132.

Put It in Writing

Take another look at the photo at the start of this chapter. Pretend you are speaking to a reporter. Write a short narrative sentence or two to answer her questions. Be sure to use helping verbs in all your answers.

1. What do the rescue workers need to do?

____

____

____

2. Should the onlookers do anything?

____

____

____

3. What would you do, if you were in charge of the rescue operation?

____

____

____

Unit 1 Mastery Review

In this Unit, we have looked at ways to write sentences that tell about the time of an action. Now, see how well you have mastered these skills, which are so important in narrative writing.

Show What You Know

Use words from the following list to complete this story. Remember that verb forms are very important if you want to write a clear narrative. And the right helping word can make the meaning of a verb clearer, too. After you have filled in all seven blank spaces, write two or three more sentences to finish the story.

eat	choke	should	learn
talk	do	come	catch

[1]Last night, I was really glad I ________________ first aid. [2]Joe and I ________________ at a new restaurant. [3]"I ________________ here all the time," said Joe. [4]That was his big mistake: He ________________ with his mouth full. [5]Joe started ________________ on a bone that was ________________ in his throat. [6]I knew what a person ________________ in just such a situation.

____

____

____

____

____

Compare your answers with ours on page 132.

Put It in Writing

Now, take another good look at the photos that started this Unit. There seems to be a story behind each picture. When you started this Unit, you were asked to write a few "key words" for each picture. Write a short narrative for each photo, using some of the key words you selected.

In one narrative, write at least three sentences: one in the past tense, another in the present tense, and a third in one of the future tenses. In another narrative, use the progressive tenses. In your third narrative, use the helping words you learned.

Finally, remember your last assignment at the start of this Unit. You were asked to write "key words" about your own life. Try to use some of the "key words" you wrote down then, when you write your fourth narrative, called "A True Story."

Photo 1 (Use Simple Past, Simple Present, Simple Future)

____

____

____

Photo 2 (Use Progressive Tenses)

____

____

____

Photo 3 (Use Helping Words)

____

____

____

A True Story

____

____

____

Music Hall RADIO CITY Music Hall RADIO CITY

UNIT 2

Writing Clear Sentences

In Unit 1 we talked about the purposes of writing. We said that one purpose for writing is to tell a narrative story. Another important purpose is to give opinions, to convince your readers about something. This type of writing is called **persuasive.**

In persuasive writing, you could give your opinion on a proposed increase in bus fare. You could argue why you deserve a promotion. Or you could say why you think the 55-mph speed limit should be raised.

A newspaper review of a movie is persuasive writing. Such reviews, or criticisms, of movies, books, or concerts, are examples of persuasive writing. In a review, you are saying why you like or don't like something. The why in persuasive writing is important: You need to give reasons for your opinion.

Advertising is also persuasive. Commercials and advertisements list reasons why you should buy a particular product or think a particular way.

In persuasive writing, you need to present your opinions clearly. This unit will help you learn some grammar rules, so that you can write sentences your readers will understand.

Before You Begin

Put an X in the box next to the answer that best completes the sentence.

If you want to write something persuasive, you will try

- ☐ a. to make a scene so real, the reader can almost "see" and "hear" the things you describe.
- ☐ b. to make your opinion seem so convincing that it will change another person's views.
- ☐ c. to tell a story in clear and interesting language.
- ☐ d. to teach your reader how to do something as clearly as you can.

If you put an X in the box next to b, you were correct. Although persuasive writing may include descriptions, and it may tell a story or teach something, too, it is first of all meant to convince the reader that your opinion is the right one.

Brainstorming

Take another look at the photos that started this Unit. You probably have an opinion about the things shown in these photos.

In the spaces below, write some "key words" for each of the photos. Look for words that could help you give your opinion about the things you see in the photos. This time, you're not chosing words to write a narrative. You are not trying to tell a story: You are trying to be persuasive.

After you have chosen your key words for the photos, find a few more key words that could help you give your opinion about something that really happened to you or to someone you know.

As in Unit 1, you'll use these key words after you've mastered the lessons in Unit 2, so choose them well!

Photo 1: ____

Photo 2: ____

Photo 3: ____

It's Only My Opinion, but: ______________________________

CHAPTER 4

Writing Verbs to Agree with Subjects

These people feel very strongly about a number of things. They are against certain things, and they want certain other things very much. They are demonstrating for their opinions. Do you agree with their method of expressing their views?

As you learned in the last unit, verbs change their form in some tenses because of the subject of the verb. This is called making the verb "agree with" its subject. Matching the right form of a verb to the subject is called **subject-and-verb agreement.**

For instance, the subjects I, he, she, and it—or words that can replace them—are called **singular subjects.** A singular subject names only one person, place, or thing. You must use the singular form of a verb to agree with a singular subject.

The subjects we and they—or words that can replace them—are called **plural subjects.** Plural subjects name more than one person, place, or thing. You must use the plural form of a verb to agree with a plural subject.

Exceptions: The subject you could be either singular or plural in meaning. That is, you could name one person or more than one person. However, in English, the plural form of a verb is always used with you. (Remember: You are the one.)

LESSON 8: Checking Agreement with the It-versus-They Test

You can use the basic knowledge you now have to solve many problems of subject-and-verb agreement. Can you use he, she, or it instead of the subject? If so, the subject is singular and takes a singular verb form. Can you use we or they instead of the subject? Then the subject is plural and takes a plural verb form.

Try It Out

Try this method with the following sentences. Place an X in the box in front of the way you would rewrite these sentences:

1. Six dollars (is, are) too much to charge for a ticket.
   - ☐ It is too much to charge for a ticket.
   - ☐ They are too much to charge for a ticket.
2. Two weeks (is, are) not enough time for a vacation.
   - ☐ It is not enough time for a vacation.
   - ☐ They are not enough time for a vacation.

In both of these sentences, the subject could be replaced by it. Subjects that name an amount of something as one thing are singular. They need a singular verb. So, you must use the singular verb is in both of these examples.

In Your Own Words

Give an opinion, using each of the following subjects. Write your sentences in the present tense. Check for subject-and-verb agreement.

1. One hundred miles ______________________________.
2. Two months ______________________________.
3. Three hundred pounds ______________________________.

Compare your sentences with those on page 132.

A. Singular Subjects That Look Like Plurals

Sometimes subject-and-verb agreement in the English language can get tricky. Some singular subjects look like plurals.

Try It Out

Place an X in the box in front of the way you would rewrite these sentences:

1. Politics (is, are) not my favorite subject.
   - ☐ It is not my favorite subject.
   - ☐ They are not my favorite subject.
2. The measles (is, are) a common childhood disease.
   - ☐ It is a common childhood disease.
   - ☐ They are a common childhood disease.

In both of these sentences, the subject could be replaced by it. Most plural words end with an -s, but some singular words also end with the letter s. Politics names one subject, and measles names one disease. These words just happen to be spelled with a final s. But both subjects in these examples take is, which is the singular form of the verb be.

Here is a list of words that end with an s. All of these words are singular. They would all need a singular form of a verb for correct agreement.

athletics	mathematics	gymnastics
measles	economics	news
mumps	physics	politics
molasses	electronics	United States

In Your Own Words

Use any three of the words in the list just given as the subjects of sentences of your own. Use the present tense. Check for subject-and-verb agreement.

1. ______________________________

______________________________.

2. ______________________________

______________________________.

3. ______________________________

______________________________.

Compare your sentences with those on page 132.

B. Singular Subjects That Take the Plural Form of the Verb

There are a few words that name only one thing but that we talk about with plural verbs and pronouns.

Try It Out

Here are some examples of this confusing problem. Place an X in the box in front of the way you would rewrite these sentences.

1. The scissors (is, are) on the table.
   - ☐ It is on the table.
   - ☐ They are on the table.
2. His new glasses (makes, make) his eyes look bigger.
   - ☐ It makes his eyes look bigger.
   - ☐ They make his eyes look bigger.
3. Your jeans (was, were) very faded.
   - ☐ It was very faded.
   - ☐ They were very faded.

All of these subjects take the plural form of the verb. The answers are <u>are</u>, <u>make</u>, and <u>were</u>. To remember that these words take plural verbs, remember that they all name something that comes in a <u>pair</u>.

In Your Own Words

Write three sentences of your own with these same three subjects—scissors, glasses, and jeans. Check for subject-and-verb agreement.

1. ____________________

2. ____________________

3. ____________________

Compare your sentences with those on page 132.

LESSON 9: Finding the Simple Subject to Check Agreement

The test we have been using can also be helpful when there are many words added to the subject.

Try It Out

Place an X in the box in front of the way you would rewrite these sentences.

1. The cause of all these problems **(is, are)** not known.
   - ☐ It is not known.
   - ☐ They are not known.
2. Those large, red books on the shelf **(looks, look)** important.
   - ☐ It looks important.
   - ☐ They look important.

In the first sentence, it is the cause (singular subject) that is (singular verb) not known. In the second sentence, it is the books (plural subject) that look (plural verb) important. The words that are around the subject do not affect subject-and-verb agreement. These words are not the subject of the sentences.

The words cause and books are called the **simple subjects** of these sentences. The simple subject of a sentence is the key word or words telling what the sentence is about. The verb always agrees with the simple subject, not with any descriptions or other added words.

In Your Own Words

Fill in the blanks in the following sentences. You may use any verbs that make sense. Check for subject-and-verb agreement.

1. The cause for all the floods ________________ clear to me.
2. The story about your aunt and uncle still ________________ me.
3. The scenes in the movie ________________ too dramatic.

Compare your answers with those on page 132.

A. Finding the Subject in Sentences Beginning with Here and There

In questions and in sentences that begin with here or there, you will not find the simple subject in front of the verb. You can locate the simple subject by rewriting. Then you can decide on correct subject-and-verb agreement.

Try It Out

For each of the following examples, we will show you how you would rewrite the questions and sentences. Place an X in the box in front of the correct meaning of each rewrite:

1. Where (is, are) the keys to the car?
   Rewrite as: The keys to the car **(is, are)** where?
   ☐ It is where?
   ☐ They are where?
2. Why (doesn't, don't) your front door bell work?
   Rewrite as: Your front door bell **(don't, doesn't)** work—why?
   ☐ It doesn't work.
   ☐ They don't work.
3. Here (is, are) the answer to my prayers.
   Rewrite as: The answer to my prayers **(is, are)** here.
   ☐ It is here.
   ☐ They are here.
4. There (goes, go) one of the happiest men in the world.
   Rewrite as: One of the happiest men in the world **(goes, go)** there.
   ☐ He goes there.
   ☐ They go there.

Sentence 1 has a plural simple subject—keys. The correct verb is are. Sentences 2, 3, and 4 have singular simple subjects—bell, answer, and one. The correct verbs are doesn't, is, and goes.

In Your Own Words

Write four sentences of your own. Start them with the words we give you. Check for subject-and-verb agreement.

1. What ____

____?

2. When ____

____?

3. Here ____

____.

4. There ____

____.

Compare your sentences with those on page 133.

LESSON 10: Checking Agreement with Compound Subjects

The simple subjects of the sentences we have looked at so far have been only one word. In some sentences, two or more subjects share the same verb. We call such subjects **compound subjects.** The words that join the parts of the compound together make a difference in how you solve subject-and-verb agreement problems.

A. Subjects Joined with And

When you use the word and to join two or more subjects together, you can use the it-versus-they test.

Try It Out

Place an X in the box in front of the way you would rewrite these sentences:

1. Juan, Mark, and Fred (is, are) voting for the strike.
   - ☐ He is voting for the strike.
   - ☐ They are voting for the strike.
2. Romeo and Juliet (is, are) a touching love story.
   - ☐ It is a touching love story.
   - ☐ They are a touching love story.
3. Spaghetti and meatballs (is, are) the only dish on the menu that I like.
   - ☐ It is the only dish on the menu that I like.
   - ☐ They are the only dish on the menu that I like.

In the first sentence, the subject could be replaced by they. This compound has a plural meaning and takes the plural verb are. In the last two sentences, the subjects could be replaced by it. The word and is not a signal for a compound subject naming more than one person, place, or thing. These subjects name only one thing and thus get singular verbs. So, the correct verbs are was and is.

B. Subjects Joined with Either ... or, Neither ... nor, or Not only ..., but also

When you use one of these three pairs of words to join the parts of a compound subject, the verb must agree with the part of the compound that is closer to the verb. It will take practice to remember this rule.

Try It Out

Fill in the blanks of the explanations of the following sentences.

1. Either Fred or Margo (**is, are**) going to win this election.

   The subject part closer to the verb is ____________________.

   This subject part is (**singular, plural**) ____________________.

   So the correct verb form is ________________.

2. Neither the boss nor the workers (**is, are**) happy about the strike.

The subject part closer to the verb is ______.

This subject part is (**singular, plural**) ______.

So the correct verb form is ______.

3. Not only our prices but also our quality (**draws, draw**) people into our store.

The subject part closer to the verb is ______.

This subject part is (**singular, plural**) ______.

So the correct verb form is ______.

In sentence 1, the singular word Margo is the subject part that is closer to the verb. The verb must be the singular form is. In sentence 2, the plural word workers is the subject part that is closer to the verb. The verb must be the plural form are. In sentence 3, the singular word quality is the subject part that is closer to the verb. The verb must be the singular form draws.

In Your Own Words

Give your opinion for each of the following subjects and complete each sentence. Be careful about subject-and-verb agreement.

1. My mother and father ______
______.

2. Either pollution or cigarettes ______
______.

3. Neither the President nor his aides ______
______.

4. Religion and politics ______
______.

5. Not only his temper, but also his habits ______
______.

Compare your sentences with those on page 133.

LESSON 11: Special Problems in Subject-and-Verb Agreement

There are four groups of words that give writers the greatest number of problems with subject-and-verb agreement. The it-versus-they test we have been using won't always help you decide how to work with the subjects in these four groups.

A. Subjects That Always Take Singular Verbs

Pronouns that name a group of people or things as one whole group always take the singular form of the verb. This includes pronouns that end with -one, -body, or -thing.

everyone	everybody	everything
someone	somebody	something
no one	nobody	nothing
anyone	anybody	anything
one	—	—

Try It Out

Circle the correct form of the verb in the following sentences:

1. Somebody **(needs, need)** to do it.
2. Nothing **(seems, seem)** to help.
3. Everybody **(thinks, think)** you're great.
4. **(Does, Do)** anybody know you're here?
5. One of us **(has, have)** a problem.
6. Here **(is, are)** everything you'll need.

Since somebody, nothing, everyone, one, anybody, and everything are pronouns that name a group of people or things as a whole group, all the sentences take the singular form of the verb: needs, seems, thinks, Does, has, and is.

Words that name a group of people or things acting as though they were one take the singular form of the verb, too. These are called **collective nouns.**

army	crowd	orchestra
audience	band	mob
class	family	nation
committee	group	public
company	herd	staff
crew	jury	team

Try It Out

Circle the correct form of the verb in the following sentences:

1. The audience **(is, are)** leaving.
2. The jury **(wants, want)** to see the gun.
3. My family **(thinks, think)** I'm crazy.
4. The public **(has, have)** a right to know.
5. Here **(comes, come)** the angry crowd.
6. **(Is, Are)** the staff in the office friendly?

Since audience, jury, family, public, crowd, and staff are words that name a group of people who are acting as though they were one, all the sentences take the singular form of the verb: is, wants, thinks, has, comes, and Is.

B. Subjects That Always Take Plural Verbs

The following pronouns always name more than one person, place, or thing:

both few many several

Try It Out

Circle the correct form of the verb in the following sentences:

1. Both **(looks, look)** good on you.
2. Few **(wants, want)** to die.
3. Several of the plants **(needs, need)** water.

Since the pronouns that are the subjects of these sentences always name more than one person, place, or thing, all three sentences take the plural form of the verb: look, want, and need.

C. Subjects That Can Be Either Singular or Plural

Some words help you name part of some whole. When that whole is one thing, the subject is singular. When that whole is made up of several things, the subject is plural. Such words include the following:

all part any some half most none

Try It Out

Circle the correct form of the verb in the following sentences:

1. All of this nightmare **(is, are)** over.
2. All of my friends **(is, are)** going.
3. Half of that pizza **(is, are)** mine.
4. Half of these vegetables **(is, are)** rotten.
5. Most of the evening **(was, were)** fine.
6. Most of the men **(was, were)** nice.

In sentences 1, 3, and 5, the subject is about one thing: nightmare, pizza, and evening. So the pronoun that is the subject of the sentences (All, Half, and Most) takes the singular form of the verb. In sentences 2, 4, and 6, we have the same pronouns for the subject of each sentence, but friends, vegetables, and men name more than one person or thing. So these sentences take the plural form of the verb.

In Your Own Words

Give your opinion for each of the following subjects. Check subject-and-verb agreement.

1. Nothing in that store ______________________________

____.

2. Most of the people in the United States ______________________________

____.

3. My favorite team ______________________________

____.

4. Anyone who believes in astrology ______________________________

____.

5. Both of those sweaters ______________________________________

____.

Compare your sentences with those on page 133.

Check Your Skills: Check Agreement with the It-versus-They Test

Circle the correct verb forms in the following sentences.

1. Electronics (**is, are**) going to be very useful in my career.
2. Ten dollars (**is, are**) not enough to get us through the weekend.
3. Thanks for your scissors. My scissors (**needs, need**) to be sharpened.
4. Bad news (**travels, travel**) fast.
5. Twenty pounds (**is, are**) too much weight to lose in one week.
6. Gymnastics (**is, are**) a difficult sport.
7. Fifty years (**is, are**) a long time to be married.
8. Jeans (**is, are**) too casual to wear to school.

Check your answers on page 133.

Check Your Skills: Find Simple Subjects to Solve Subject-and-Verb Agreement

Circle the correct verb form in the following sentences.

1. The source for all these newspaper articles on love and understanding (**was, were**) not given.
2. There (**stands, stand**) the one person who can help us all.
3. My idea of going out and enjoying myself (**is, are**) different from yours.
4. Here (**is, are**) the names of the people I cut from the wedding invitation list.
5. How (**was, were**) the people in your office planning to celebrate your birthday?

Check your answers on page 133.

Check Your Skills: Check Subject-and-Verb Agreement with Compound Subjects

Circle the correct verb form in the following sentences.

1. This coat and tie (**looks, look**) good together.
2. Bacon and eggs (**is, are**) my favorite breakfast.
3. Neither my brother nor my sisters (**is, are**) coming to my wedding.
4. Either you or your wife (**is, are**) telling me a lie.
5. Not only their broken-down cars but also their poor service record (**makes, make**) them the worst used car dealers in town.

Check your answers on page 133.

Check Your Skills: Check Subjects and Verbs for Agreement

For each of the following sentences, fill in the chart. Find the simple subject and put it in the first column of the chart. In the second column, tell whether the simple subject needs a singular or a plural verb. Use an S for singular and a P for plural. Finally, in the third column, fill in the verb that will agree with the subject. There is an example to show you how to fill in the chart.

	Simple Subject	Singular or Plural	Verb
Example: Water at sea level (**boils, boil**) at 212°.	*water*	*S*	*boils*
1. His blue pants (**needs, need**) ironing.	_______	____	____
2. The cause of your headaches (**seems, seem**) obvious.	_______	____	____
3. Where (**is, are**) the money I gave you?	_______	____	____
4. Fred and his mother (**thinks, think**) Alice is wrong.	_______	____	____
5. The orchestra (**is, are**) about to play.	_______	____	____
6. Here (**is, are**) the books you wanted.	_______	____	____
7. Everyone (**has, have**) a reason for living.	_______	____	____

	Simple Subject	Singular or Plural	Verb
8. Both (**costs, cost**) far too much money.	______	____	____
9. Either Sara or her parents (**is, are**) driving out to get you.	______	____	____
10. Half of that movie (**gives, give**) me the chills even now.	______	____	____
11. Two tablespoons (**was, were**) too much salt to add.	______	____	____
12. The United States (**has, have**) not always been blameless in war.	______	____	____
13. The scissors (**is, are**) too dull for cutting hair.	______	____	____
14. The effects of violence on television and in the movies (**is, are**) hotly debated.	______	____	____
15. When (**does, do**) the children take a nap?	______	____	____
16. Neither Tim nor his wife (**wants, want**) the divorce.	______	____	____
17. My favorite team (**loses, lose**) every game.	______	____	____
18. There (**is, are**) the man you were talking about.	______	____	____
19. Somebody (**needs, need**) to watch the baby.	______	____	____
20. Some of my teachers (**thinks, think**) I'm very smart.	______	____	____
21. Twenty miles (**is, are**) too far to walk.	______	____	____
22. Mathematics (**is, are**) hard for me to understand.	______	____	____
23. The Beatles (**sings, sing**) my favorite song from the sixties.	______	____	____
24. One of you (**is, are**) not telling the whole truth.	______	____	____
25. Most of the food (**was, were**) delicious.	______	____	____

Check your answers on page 134.

Put It in Writing

Write at least three sentences on each of the following subjects. Try to use amount subjects, compound subjects, either . . . or, neither . . . nor, not only, . . . but also, and the special agreement problem words on pages 50–52.

1. Sports in high schools—can we get along without them?
2. The fees doctors are charging—must it be this way?
3. Look your best—dieting or exercise?

Put It in Writing

Write at least three sentences. Give your opinion about the photo at the start of this chapter. Make the subject of one sentence the marchers. Make the subject of another sentence the group. Use either . . . or, neither . . . nor, or not only, . . . but also in a third sentence. Then continue giving your opinion, if you wish.

CHAPTER 5

Writing with Pronouns

What do you think about this mess! It's something you can see almost any day in a big city. Someday, there might be "gridlock," and then nobody will be going anywhere! If there were no private cars in our cities, though, would things be better or worse for everybody?

When you checked for subject-and-verb agreement in Chapter 4, we suggested that you try replacing the subject with the pronouns he and they. In your own writing, you often use these and other pronouns. They help you avoid repeating the same noun over and over. The following two paragraphs show just how important this can be.

Try It Out

In the second paragraph, we have replaced the underlined words with pronouns. How many different kinds of pronouns do you find in the second paragraph?

John smokes two packs of cigarettes a day. John has smoked for almost thirty years. John's doctor told John to stop smoking altogether. The cigarette smoke wasn't good for John. John was developing a bad early-morning cough.

John smokes two packs of cigarettes a day. He has smoked for almost thirty years. His doctor told him to stop smoking altogether. The cigarette smoke wasn't good for him. He was developing a bad early-morning cough.

In our paragraph, there were three different pronouns used to replace John's name—he, him, and his. After we used John once, it became awkward to keep repeating the name. You probably use pronouns for this same purpose without even thinking about it. But how can you be sure that you are using the right pronoun forms? The answer lies in understanding the different kinds of work that words do in a sentence. Under the rules of grammar, you choose pronoun forms depending on the work your pronouns are doing.

LESSON 12: Checking for Subjects and Direct Objects

In the previous chapters, you have matched subjects and verbs. You have used the words he, she, and it as singular subjects, and we and they as plural subjects. I, he, she, it, you, we, and they are **subject pronouns.** They tell who or what the sentence is about.

John smokes.
He smokes.
Who smokes? (He stands for John.)

Try It Out

Use a pronoun in place of the underlined subject.

1. Many workers signed the petition. ________
2. The ceremony was impressive. ________
3. My husband and I wrote a letter to the editor. ________
4. Rita is looking for a new job. ________
5. Jack will be getting a complete physical. ________

Check your answers on page 134.

Some sentences are complete with only a subject and a verb. But some verbs name an action that can only be done to someone or something. When you use these verbs, you need to answer the questions Who? or What?

John smokes cigarettes.

John smokes them.

What does John smoke? (them stands for cigarettes.)

A word that answers the questions Whom? or What? after a verb is called a **direct object.** Me, him, her, it, you, us, and them are **object pronouns.**

Try It Out

Use a pronoun in place of the underlined direct object.

1. We urge the senators to vote against the bill. ________
2. The judge sentenced Tony to a year in jail. ________
3. The store guarantees this TV. ________
4. We will be meeting Linda after the show. ________
5. Do you remember Lee and me? ________

Check your answers on page 134.

In Your Own Words

Practice giving opinions. Complete the following sentences in your own words. Notice that subjects and direct objects have been given.

1. I like ____

   ____.

2. We need ____

   ____.

3. ______________________________ help(s) us because

   ____.

4. ______________________________ surprises me.

5. ______________________________, so buy them.

Compare your sentences with those on page 134.

LESSON 13: Checking for Indirect Objects

You know that object pronouns are used as direct objects. Now you will learn that these pronouns have another important use. They can name the person to whom or for whom the action of the sentence is done.

A word that answers the questions To whom? or For whom? or To What? or For What? after a verb is called an **indirect object**. Indirect objects can only appear in a sentence that also has a direct object.

Here is an example of the difference between direct and indirect objects:

He gave me his opinion.
What did he give? His opinion.
This is the **direct object.**

To whom did he give it? Me.
This is the **indirect object.**

Try It Out

Try identifying direct and indirect objects in the following sentences. Tell how the underlined pronouns are being used. Place an X in the box under the correct column.

If you're not sure about the answer, ask questions like the one under the first sentence.

	Direct Object	**Indirect Object**
1. He bought them some flowers. What did he bring? *flowers* To whom did he bring this? *them*	☐	☐
2. I wrote you and him a letter.	☐	☐
3. They asked her some questions.	☐	☐
4. We found him a new job.	☐	☐

All of the underlined pronouns were indirect objects. All of them tell to whom or for whom the action was done. Because they were indirect objects, we used the object pronoun forms. The direct objects in these sentences were some flowers, a letter, some questions, and a new job. These are the words that answer the question Who? or What? after the verb in each sentence.

In Your Own Words

Try writing your own sentences with pronouns as indirect objects. Use the verb together with the correct form of the pronouns given in parentheses. You can use any verb tense you like. Use questions to check your sentences for direct and indirect objects.

Example: (get—she, her) *Somebody should get her a gift.*
(**Check:** What should somebody get? *A gift*
This is the **direct object.**
For whom should someone get this? *her*
This is the **indirect object.**)

1. (give—he, him) ______________________________

2. (send—I, me) ______________________________

3. (read—they, them) ______________________________

LESSON 14: Checking Pronouns Used with Prepositions

Direct and indirect objects add important information to your sentences. But in some sentences, you may want to add a noun or pronoun with a special kind of word called a **preposition.** The preposition can show your readers a connection that direct and indirect objects cannot show.

Try It Out

Here are some examples of sentences in which pronouns have been added using a preposition. Underline the pronouns. Circle the word that connects the pronoun to another word in the sentence. This connecting word is a preposition.

The secret between us is no secret anymore.

Ted wouldn't look behind him.

The Johnsons always have children around them.

Bette knows the truth about me.

The cat just stared at her.

You circled the words between, behind, around, about, and at. All of these words are prepositions. As you can see, they can give your readers many different kinds of information. The preposition plus the words it connects to the sentence are called a **prepositional phrase.** The noun or pronoun in the phrase is called the **object of the preposition.**

Try It Out

Look back at our example sentences above. Write all the pronouns you find on the line below.

____

You wrote the pronouns us, him, them, me, and her. All of these pronouns are object pronouns. As the name implies, a pronoun used as the object of a preposition must be an object pronoun.

In Your Own Words

Write three sentences of your own. Use the prepositions given in parentheses. Use an object pronoun after the preposition.

Example: (about) *The doctors were talking about him.*

1. (on) ________________

2. (from) ________________

3. (with) ________________

Compare your sentences with those on page 135.

Check Your Skills: Write the Correct Forms of Pronouns

Fill in the blanks with the correct form of a pronoun.

Dear John,

[1]You and ________ must face facts. [2]You did give ________ many good times. [3]But ________ can no longer say, "________ are lucky people." [4]Please don't hate ________. [5]But it is over between you and ________.

Judy

Dear Mark,

[6]I'd like you and your wife to keep an eye on John for ________. [7]I know you can help ________ through this. [8]After all, you and ________ are such good friends. [9]Your wife could invite ________ for dinner to make sure ________ eats. [10]Together, you and ________ can help John in many ways. [11]Thank your wife from both of ________. [12]I don't know what we'd do without you and ________.

Judy

Dear Judy,

[13]Your letter to Mark and Helen saddens ________. [14]I had dinner with ________ last night. [15]You gave ________ a lot to talk about. [16]________ want to be a foursome again. [17]Both ________ and ________ want to see ________ together again. [18]As a foursome, our evenings together gave both ________ and ________ such pleasure. [19]I can't think that you're happy without ________.

John

Check your answers on page 135.

Put It in Writing

Take another look at the photo at the start of this chapter. Do you think this picture shows a problem? Or are some people making a fuss over nothing? If it shows a problem, what should be done? Have your say, and use as many clear pronouns as possible. Circle all the pronouns when you are done.

____

____

____

____

____

____

____

____

____

Unit 2 Mastery Review

In this Unit we have looked at ways to make the parts of a sentence "agree." You have seen that when the subject is just one person or just one thing, the verb that names the action of the subject has to be singular, too. When the subject is more than just one person or thing, the verb must "agree" with the subject by being in the plural form. You've seen, too, that sometimes it isn't so easy to know right away whether the subject is singular or plural.

You have also learned how to replace a noun with the correct pronoun form. You have seen how important it is that you show whether the pronoun replaces a direct object or an indirect object. And you have worked with pronouns that follow prepositions, too.

Now you'll have a chance to use all of the skills you have mastered so far in Units 1 and 2.

Show What You Know

Use words from the following list to complete this paragraph. Be sure to check for subject-and-verb agreement. After you have filled in all the blank spaces, write two or three sentences to give an opinion on the topic, the way you'd do it.

claim	be	ask	have
look	fill	do	want

[1]Everyone I know ________________ a plan to help me lose weight. [2]To be honest, my pants ________________ not fit me quite the way they used to. [3]One of my friends ________________ her diet can't fail. [4]She tells me that 800 calories a day ________________ her up fine. [5]Dry toast and lettuce ________________ hamster food, I tell her. [6]My family ________________ me to run five miles every day! [7]Well, five blocks ________________ far enough to me!

[8]Nobody ____________ for my opinion on this subject, of course.

Fill in the blank spaces in the following paragraph, using the correct pronoun forms. Then write two or three more sentences of your own, giving your opinion on the subject of "smart shopping."

[1]Last night, my friends and ________ were talking about how we saved money at the supermarket. [2]Carla said we could all learn something from ________ . [3]________ saves coupons for soap and food. [4]She gets a lot of her coupons from the rest of my friends and ________ , in fact! [5]Ted compares the ads for all the supermarkets near ________ . [6]His wife and ________ take a lot of time to make up a shopping list. [7]It's worth it to ________ . [8]________ save a lot of money by buying their food on sale.

Compare your answers with ours on page 135.

Put It in Writing

Turn back now to the start of this Unit. The photos there were chosen because people have strong opinions about the topics the pictures suggest. You were asked to list key words on the subjects shown in the pictures. Take another look at those words.

Using some or all of your key words, write at least one persuasive sentence for each photo. Do you think the photo shows something that's fine the way it is? Or does it show something that needs to be changed? If you think the photo shows something that is a problem, maybe you can suggest ways the situation could be improved.

Be aware of verb tenses. Something may have been better in the old days than it is now. Or maybe it used to be worse. Maybe you think it has to get better in the future. The correct verb form and the right helping word will help you persuade your reader.

After you have written about the photos, write at least one more sentence on a topic you feel strongly about. Use at least some of the key words you wrote down at the start of this Unit.

Photo 1 ____

____

____

Photo 2 ____

____

____

Photo 3 ____

____

____

It's My Opinion ____

____

____

____

$1.98
BEEF BONUS
PAK SECTION
PORK BONUS
PAK SECTION

UNIT 3

Writing Descriptive Sentences

Perhaps the most common reason you write is to describe something. With words you can create pictures of people and places, actions and feelings. You can describe the world around you, paint a picture of the past, or take people into a make-believe time and place.

In your everyday writing you can write descriptions. You can tell a friend what each member of your family is like, what they look like and how they act. You can describe your neighborhood. You can write about the way your neighbors look or how they act. You can also note the different ways people act at a ball game, or at a family get-together, or in a restaurant. You can jot down how you feel when you meet someone you like or when you have an argument. All of this is descriptive writing.

Look through books and you'll find many examples of descriptive writing—descriptions of characters' behavior or appearance, word pictures of places and situations. Flip through a newspaper or a magazine and you'll find ads describing how products taste or look or how they make you feel or look when you buy them.

In this unit, you'll look at how to use the most common describing words: adjectives and adverbs.

Before You Begin

Put an X in the box next to the answer that best completes the sentence.

Descriptive writing is used

☐ a. to convince the reader that your opinion is the right one.
☐ b. to tell a story as clearly as possible.
☐ c. to help the reader "see," "hear," and "feel" something the way you yourself did.
☐ d. to teach the reader how to build something, step by step.

If you put an X in the box next to c, you are ready to try your hand at descriptive writing. A good description makes your writing come "alive." Narrative writing and persuasive writing are both helped by clear and lively description.

Brainstorming

Take another look at the photos that started this unit. Each photo gives you something to describe.

In the spaces below, write at least one key word for each photo. A key word could be a verb, talking about the action shown in the photo. Or it could be a noun, identifying someone or something shown. But in this Unit we are looking for words that describe. So be sure to look for words that give you a sense of the mood, the speed, the sounds, and colors of the scenes.

After you have written in the key words for the photos, write another key word or two on the fourth line. This is for something you've really seen or heard in your own life. Maybe it's something you are looking at or listening to right now.

As in Units 1 and 2, you'll use these key words at the end of this Unit, after you've mastered the lessons in Chapters 6 through 8.

Photo 1: ____

Photo 2: ____

Photo 3: ____

I See or Hear It Clearly Now: ____________________________

CHAPTER 6

Descriptive Writing with Adjectives and Adverbs

Kids cooling off and just having fun making noise! If you had to describe this scene for someone who couldn't see the photo, what details would you choose? What different verbs would you need to make this scene "come alive"?

You know that you can write meaningful statements by putting verbs together with nouns or pronouns as subjects and objects. However, the nouns, pronouns, and verbs you use often don't give your readers as clear a picture as you want.

For any noun or pronoun, you may want to add words to tell your readers more about that person, place, or thing. For example, the noun men by itself won't tell your readers **how many** men or **what kind** of men.

Try It Out

Fill in the blanks with the words we added to describe the nouns in the following sentence.

The men talked to the boss.
The seven strange men talked to the new boss.

how many men? ____________

what kind of men? ____________

what kind of boss? ____________

The words you filled in the blanks are **adjectives.** Adjectives are words used to describe people, places, things, or ideas. That is, adjectives describe nouns or pronouns.

For any action verb you use, you may want to add words to tell something more about the action. For example, the action verb talked by itself won't tell your readers **how, when, how often, how long,** or **where** someone talked.

Try It Out

Fill in the blanks with the words from the sentences that answer the questions. All of these words describe the action shown by the verb talked.

Sue talked to her children.

Sue talked softly to her children.	talked **how?**	____________
Sue talked to her children yesterday.	talked **when?**	____________
Sue always talked to her children.	talked **how often?**	____________

Sue talked endlessly to her children. talked **how long?** ____________

Sue talked to her children outside. talked **where?** ____________

The words you filled in the blanks are **adverbs.** Adverbs are words used to describe action verbs.

LESSON 15: Telling the Difference between Adjectives and Adverbs

Adjectives and adverbs are very useful tools for writers. But adjectives and adverbs do different kinds of work in a sentence. With a few exceptions, you can't use exactly the same word to do these different kinds of work. You must show the difference.

Try It Out

The following examples show what may happen to an adjective when it is used as an adverb. Fill in the blanks in the explanations. The first one is done for you, as an example.

1. That horrible performer sang a ballad.
   The word horrible tells **what kind** of *performer*.
   That performer sang a horrible ballad.
   The word horrible tells **what kind** of *ballad*.
   That performer sang a ballad horribly.
   The word horribly tells **how** the performer *sang*.

2. The lazy clerk yawned.

   The word lazy tells **what kind** of ____________.

   The clerk yawned lazily.

   The word lazily tells **how** the clerk ____________.

3. The hard ball hit her.

   The word hard tells **what kind** of ____________.

   The ball hit her hard.

   The word hard tells **how** the ball ____________ her.

In the first two sentences, the ending -ly was added to the adjectives horrible and lazy to form adverbs. The adjective horrible described the nouns performer and ballad. But the form of the word changes to horribly when it became an adverb describing the verb sang. The adjective lazy described the noun clerk. But the form of the word changed to lazily when it became an adverb describing the verb yawned. Most adverbs, like horribly and lazily, are formed by adding -ly to the adjective.

In the last example, the form of hard did not change. The word stayed the same whether it described the noun ball or the verb hit. The word hard can be either an adjective or an adverb.

See how much you already know about changing the form of an adjective when you need an adverb. Refer to the spelling tips on page 77 if you are not sure.

Try It Out

Fill in the blanks in the following chart. Read the adjective in the first column. Use it as an adverb in the second column. Make any necessary spelling changes. The first three examples are taken from the sentences you have just been reading about.

	Adjectives			Adverbs
1.	horrible	performer	sang	horribly
2.	lazy	clerk	yawned	lazily
3.	hard	ball	hit	hard
4.	serious	problem	talked	________
5.	simple	solution	explain	________
6.	noisy	children	played	________
7.	frantic	mother	searched	________
8.	accidental	mistake	found	________
9.	fast	car	ran	________
10.	monthly	bills	paid	________
11.	understanding	person	nodded	________
12.	mistaken	identity	took	________

The correct answers are: seriously, simply, noisily, frantically, accidentally, fast, monthly, understandingly, and mistakenly. With the exception of Examples 3, 9, and 10, which remained the same, all of the adverbs were formed by adding *-ly* to the adjectives.

As you can see in Examples 11 and 12 in the chart, certain verb forms can be used as adjectives. You can use the present participle (-ing form) or the past participle of a verb as an adjective. If the verb is an irregular verb, double-check to see that you are not using the simple past form when you mean to use the past participle.

Verb: I win every game.
Adjective: She gave me a winning smile.

Verb: She forgot the answer.
Adjective: They are the forgotten people.

Verb: The boss noticed that you weren't here.
Adjective: I don't see any noticeable improvement. (You need to add the suffix -able to the verb to form an adjective.)

Adverb: Things have not improved noticeably.

Try It Out

In the first sentence in each of the following groups of sentences, the underlined word is used as a noun or a verb. Fill in the blanks in the other sentences of each group with the correct adjective or adverb form of the underlined words. Remember, the adverb is formed by adding -ly to the adjective form.

1. I was listening to some music.
   I don't play any *musical* instrument.
   The teapot whistled *musically*.

2. The children excited the animals.

   The ______________ children talked to the animals.

   The children talked ______________ to the animals.

3. The lake froze solid last night.

   The ______________ lake looked peaceful.

4. The cat broke the lamp.

   The ______________________________ lamp lay on the floor.

5. Anita is biting into a juicy steak.

   Her ______________________________ remarks make me furious.

   The wind blew ______________________________ across the bay.

6. The baby shows his anger by throwing things.

   He is often ______________________________ .

   He often throws things ______________________________ .

Check your answers on page 136.

In Your Own Words

Write a sentence for each of the following adjectives and adverbs:

1. carefully ______________________________
2. throbbing ______________________________
3. calm ______________________________
4. confused ______________________________
5. fast ______________________________
6. sleepily ______________________________

Compare your sentences with those on page 137.

As you can see, using adjectives and adverbs in your writing means checking at least two things:

1. Check to see what it is you are describing.
   a. You need an adjective to describe people, places, things, and ideas.
   b. You need an adverb to describe an action.
2. Check the spelling of the form you want.
   a. When you use a verb form as an adjective, you can use the present participle (-ing form) or the past participle. You cannot use the simple-past form.
   b. When you form an adverb by adding -ly, make sure you are adding it to the form you would use as an adjective. Then double-check for any spelling changes you need to make before adding the -ly.

Spelling Tips

1. If the adjective ends with -le, form the adverb by changing the -le to -ly.

   gentle + ly = gently   simple + ly = simply

   gentle person——touch gently
   simple solution——explain simply

2. If the adjective ends with a y, form the adverb by changing the y to an i before adding -ly.

   busy + ly = busily   greedy + ly = greedily

   busy person——worked busily
   greedy child——eat greedily

3. If the adjective ends with -ic, form the adverb by adding -ally.

   specific + ally = specifically   fantastic + ally = fantastically

   specific problem——asked specifically
   fantastic party——played fantastically

4. Some adjectives are formed by adding -al to a noun form. Remember to form the adverb by adding -ly to the adjective form, and not to the noun form.

   accidental + ly = accidentally   magical + ly = magically

   an accidental explosion——took accidentally
   a magical moment——appeared magically

5. Some adjectives and adverbs have exactly the same form.

   fast   hard   high   ill   late   long   low

   fast car——runs fast   late hours——stayed late

   early   daily   weekly   monthly   yearly

   early afternoon——arrived early
   daily newspaper——talked daily

LESSON 16: Using Linking Verbs and Adjectives

You can describe the subject of a sentence by putting an adjective right in front of it. You can fill in the blank in the following sentence with an adjective describing the subject child.

The ________________ child walked toward his mother.

Some verbs, called **linking verbs,** help you describe a subject in a different way. They act as a link between an adjective and the subject it describes. The most common linking verbs are the forms of be. In the following sentences, you can fill in an adjective to describe the subject noun child.

The child is ________________. The child is being ________________.

The child was ________________. The child was being ________________.

You must be careful with the verb be. It is not always a linking verb. It can also be a helping verb. Remember the verb tenses you studied in Chapter 2. You used forms of the verb be with the present participles (-ing forms) of a main verb. We'll add a main verb to the example sentences we just used. Now, what kind of word would you put in the blanks?

The child is screaming ________________.

The child was singing ________________.

You were right if you said that an adverb should be used in these blanks. You need an adverb to describe the actions of screaming and singing. You are no longer describing the subject noun child.

Any of the following verbs can also be linking verbs. You must be careful because most of these verbs can also name an action:

look	sound	seem	remain
smell	appear	become	stay
taste	feel	grow	

Try It Out

If the missing word describes the subject of the sentence or some other noun in the sentence, fill in the blank with the adjective form of the word in parentheses. If the missing word describes the action named by the verb, fill in the blank with the adverb form of the word in parentheses.

1. The bus driver was ____________________. **(angry, angrily)**
2. The bus driver was shouting ____________________. **(angry, angrily)**
3. The bus driver was shouting ______________ words. **(angry, angrily)**
4. The President looked ____________________. **(frantic, frantically)**
5. The President looked ____________________ through the notes on his desk. **(frantic, frantically)**
6. The child's mother grew ____________________ with him. **(impatient, impatiently)**
7. That plant certainly grew ____________________. **(quick, quickly)**
8. He appeared ____________________ in spite of his problems. **(calm, calmly)**
9. He appeared ____________________ in front of the crowd. **(sudden, suddenly)**
10. I feel ____________________ about missing your birthday. **(terrible, terribly)**

Check your answers on page 136.

Learning to spot linking verbs takes practice. But this skill will help you decide when to use adjectives or adverbs after a verb. Probably the most common decisions you make will involve the words <u>good</u>, <u>well</u>, <u>bad</u> and <u>badly</u>. These words can cause problems if you don't remember three basic rules:

1. The words <u>good</u> and <u>bad</u> are used as adjectives.
2. The word <u>badly</u> is used as an adverb.
3. The word <u>well</u> is used as an adverb. However, it can be used as an adjective if it means "in good health."

Try It Out

Fill in the blanks with the correct word given in parentheses:

1. This soup tastes ________________ . **(good, well)**
2. That suit looks ________________ on you. **(good, well)**
3. This meat smells ________________ . **(bad, badly)**
4. Things just started ________________ . **(bad, badly)**
5. I felt ________________ about my mistake. **(bad, badly)**
6. Don't you feel ________________ ? **(good, well)**
7. Your news made me feel ________________ all over. **(good, well)**
8. He plays the guitar ________________ . **(good, well)**

Check your answers on page 137.

In Your Own Words

Write four sentences using subjects, adjectives, and adverbs of your own.

1. ________________ tastes ________________ .
2. ________________ sounded ________________ .
3. ________________ seems ________________ .
4. ________________ are feeling ________________ .

Compare your sentences with those on page 138.

LESSON 17: Making Adjectives and Adverbs Stronger

You use adjectives and adverbs to help the nouns, pronouns, and verbs in your sentences clearly tell your readers who and what you are writing about. Sometimes, though, the adjectives and adverbs you use just don't seem strong enough; they don't give the full emphasis you want. You can make adjectives and adverbs stronger with adverbs.

Try It Out

Fill in the blanks in the explanations of the following sentences:

1. A dog chased my cat up a tree.
   A small dog chased my cat up a tree.
   The adjective *small* was added to describe the noun *dog*. An extremely small dog chased my cat up a tree.
   The adverb *extremely* makes the adjective *small* stronger.

2. I am honest.
   The adjective ____________ describes the subject pronoun ____________.
   I am completely honest.
   The adverb ____________ makes the adjective ____________ stronger.

3. A kind person gave me directions.
   The adjective ____________ describes the noun ____________.
   A very kind person gave me directions.
   The adverb ____________ makes the adjective ____________ stronger.

4. He moved slowly.
   The adverb ____________ describes the verb ____________.
   He moved unusually slowly.
   The adverb ____________ makes the adverb ____________ stronger.

In example 1, we first added the adjective small to describe the noun dog. Then we added the adverb extremely to make the adjective small stronger. In example 2, we used the adjective honest after a linking verb to describe the subject pronoun I. We then added the adverb completely to make the adjective honest stronger. In example 3, the noun person is described with the adjective kind. We then added the adverb very to make the adjective kind stronger. In example 4, the adverb slowly describes the verb moved. We then added the adverb unusually to make the adverb slowly stronger.

You can use any of the following adverbs in this same way:

completely	awfully	basically	so
entirely	extremely	usually	too
totally	really	unusually	
thoroughly	terribly	very	

It is important to remember to use these adverb forms. You can not use the adjective forms of these adverbs when you use them to make an adjective or another adverb stronger.

(WRONG) I had a real good time.
(RIGHT) I had a really good time.

(WRONG) They were awful nice to me.
(RIGHT) They were awfully nice to me.

The adverb really was used in front of the adjective good to make it stronger. The adverb awfully was used in front of the adjective nice to make it stronger. You could not use the adjective forms real or awful to do this kind of work.

Check Your Skills: Use Adjectives and Adverbs in Sentences

Complete the following sentences by adding the adjective form or the adverb form of the darker words in parentheses. Write your answers on the lines given.

Example: I searched for my wallet. **(frantic)**
I ***frantically*** *searched for my wallet.*

1. They repaired the leaky roof. **(busy)**

___

2. I slept last night. **(good)**

____

3. Bring it to me. **(quick)**

____

4. Cheryl is a runner. **(quick)**

____

5. She walked up to bed. **(sleepy)**

____

6. She could hardly keep her eyes open. **(sleepy)**

____

7. That was a concert! **(great)**

____

8. I have always admired him. **(great)**

____

9. I used to score on tests before I learned how to study. **(bad)**

____

10. They fought the fire for hours. **(brave)**

____

Check your answers on page 136.

Check Your Skills: Make Adjectives and Adverbs Stronger

Rewrite each of the following sentences. Add an adverb to make the underlined adjective or adverb stronger. Try to vary your adverbs.

Example: The minister's sermon was boring.
The minister's sermon was incredibly boring.

1. This stew tastes salty.

____

2. You seem happy.

____

3. They are working slowly.

____

4. You sang that song well.

____

5. The tired children were patient.

____

Compare your answers with those on page 136.

Put It in Writing

Study the photo at the start of this chapter. How many verbs would you need to describe this scene? Write a sentence for each verb. Be sure to give each verb an adverb, too. Then take another look at your sentences. Add adjectives to help liven up the nouns you used.

CHAPTER 7

Putting Adjectives and Adverbs in the Right Place

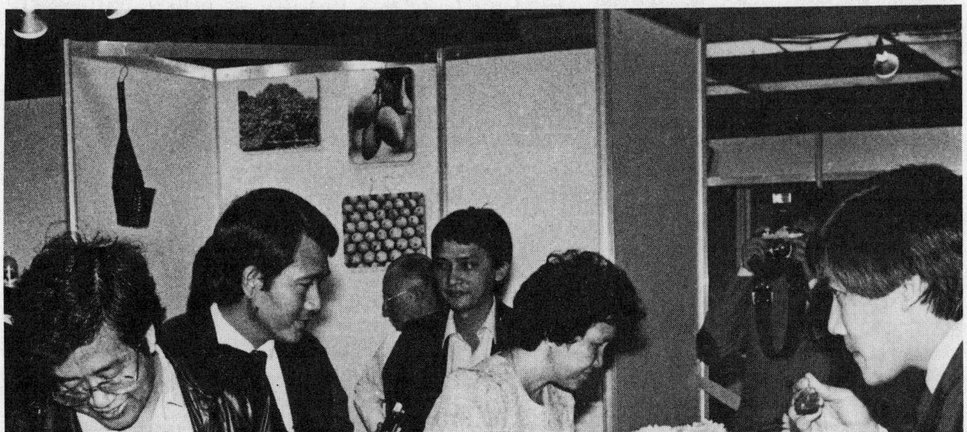

Something smells good! Could you write a description of this scene without using any adjectives or adverbs? Not likely! Can you think of four or more adjectives and adverbs that could really help you describe this get-together?

As a writer, you want to make sure your readers clearly understand what words your adjectives and adverbs describe. So, in most sentences, you try to keep adjectives and adverbs as close as possible to the nouns, pronouns, and verbs they describe.

But you also want to make sure your readers clearly understand the **main idea** of every sentence, what the sentence is about. To do that, you must think carefully about what parts of the sentence tell the main idea. This, in turn, may affect where you place your adjectives and adverbs.

In this book, you have been working with the basic ways that you can put a sentence together. As the following examples show, you state the main idea of a sentence with a subject and a verb. With some action verbs, you must add indirect and direct objects to tell the main idea. With linking verbs, you must add a word to rename or describe the subject in order to state a main idea.

Try It Out

Fill in the blanks of the explanations of the following examples. The first one has been done for you.

1. Subject + action verb

Example: The children played.
The subject is *children*
The action verb is *played*

2. Subject + action verb + direct object

Example: The boy bought a balloon.

The subject is ____________________

The action verb is ____________________

The direct object is ____________________

3. Subject + action verb + indirect object + direct object

Example: The parents gave their children love.

The subject is ____________________

The action verb is ____________________

The indirect object is ____________________

The direct object is ____________________

4. Subject + linking verb + noun or pronoun renaming the subject

   Example: One boy is a baseball player.

   The subject is ________________

   The linking verb is ________________

   The noun renaming the subject is ________________

5. Subject + linking verb + adjective describing the subject

   Example: The day was sunny.

   The subject is ________________

   The linking verb is ________________

   The adjective describing the subject is ________________

Check your answers on page 137.

You can add adjectives and adverbs to describe any of these sentence parts. But you must be careful not to add too many adjectives or adverbs between the basic sentence parts. If you do, your readers can have a difficult time finding your main idea.

LESSON 18: Adding Adjectives

Adjectives usually come right in front of the nouns they describe. But you know that an adjective can come after a linking verb to describe the subject. For special effect, you might add adjectives right after a noun.

Try It Out

Fill in the blanks of the explanations of the following examples. The first example has been done for you.

1. The old doctor watched the shiny, new machines.
   This sentence is made up of the subject *doctor*, the action verb *watched*, the direct object *machines*, plus adjectives.

The adjective ___*old*___ comes right before the subject noun ___*doctor*___.

The adjectives ___*shiny*___ and ___*new*___ come right before the direct object noun ___*machines*___.

2. The doctor was unhappy.

This sentence is made up of the subject ______________, the linking verb ______________, and the adjective ______________.

The adjective ______________ comes after the linking verb ______________, but it still describes the noun ______________.

3. The doctor, tired and unimpressed, heaved a deep sigh.

This sentence is made up of the subject ______________, the action verb ______________, the direct object ______________, plus adjectives.

The adjectives ______________ and ______________ come right after the subject noun ______________.

The adjective ______________ comes right before the direct object noun ______________.

Sentence 1 is made up of the subject doctor, the action verb watched, and the direct object machines. The adjective old describes the subject noun doctor. It comes right before the noun. So it does not get in the way of the basic sentence parts of subject + verb + direct object. The adjectives shiny and new describe the direct object noun machines. These adjectives come right before the noun, but they also come between the verb and the direct object.

It isn't hard to understand the sentence when there are two adjectives between the verb and the direct object. Adding more than two will make the sentence harder to read:

The old doctor watched the blinking, whirring, shiny, new machines.

Even with two adjectives, we added a comma to show that a second adjective followed and not the noun being described.

Sentence 2 is made up of the subject doctor, the linking verb was, and the adjective unhappy. The adjective unhappy describes the subject doctor even though it comes after the linking verb. In sentences like this, you can add quite a few adjectives. You can add them in front of the subject noun as well as after the linking verb. No matter how many you add, your readers can still easily find the basic sentence parts:

The old, gray-haired doctor was tired, annoyed, and unhappy.

Sentence 3 made up of the subject doctor, the action verb heaved, and the direct object sigh. The adjectives tired and unimpressed describe the subject noun doctor. For special effect, these adjectives were placed after the noun. The adjective deep describes the direct object noun sigh.

Even with only two adjectives, we add commas to set off the adjectives that follow immediately after the noun. This shows that these words interrupt the connection between the subject and the verb.

In Your Owns Words

Add adjectives of your own to describe the nouns in the following sentences. Add at least two adjectives to each sentence. Add commas where you need them.

1. The woman crossed the street.

____

2. The sofa looked comfortable.

____

3. The book lay open on the table.

____

Compare your sentences with those on page 137.

LESSON 19: Adding Adverbs

You can add adverbs that describe an action verb right before the verb or right after the verb. You can even put them at the beginning or at the end of the sentence as a whole. Where you choose to put an adverb will depend on two things: (1) what kind of adverb you are using, and (2) what other sentence parts you must keep together.

Try It Out

Fill in the blanks in the explanations of the following examples:

1. The door opened.

   This sentence is made up of the subject ___*door*___ and the action verb ___*opened*___.

   a. Suddenly, the door opened.
   b. The door suddenly opened.
   c. The door opened suddenly.

   The adverb ___*suddenly*___ describes the action verb ___*opened*___. It doesn't matter where you put it.

2. She dialed the number.

   This sentence is made up of the subject ______________, the action verb ______________, and the direct object ______________.

   a. Slowly, she dialed the number.
   b. She slowly dialed the number.
   c. She dialed the number slowly.

   The adverb ______________ describes the action verb ______________. The adverb clearly describes the verb in any of these positions.

   d. She dialed slowly the number.

   The adverb ______________ is placed between the ______________ and the ______________. You cannot put an adverb between these two sentence parts.

3. I can see you.

   This sentence is made up of the subject ______________, the verb helper ______________, the action verb ______________, and the direct object ______________.

a. I can almost see you.

The adverb ________________ describes the action verb ________________. The adverb clearly describes the verb when it is between the helper and the main verb.

b. Almost, I can see you.

c. I almost can see you.

d. I can see almost you.

e. I can see you almost.

In these places, the adverb makes the sentence hard to read. It does not clearly describe the action verb.

4. You are being foolish.

This sentence is made up of the subject ________________, the linking verb ________________, and the adjective ________________, which describes the subject.

a. You are being extremely foolish.

The adverb ________________ makes the adjective stronger.

It is placed right in front of the adjective.

b. Extremely, you are being foolish.

c. You extremely are being foolish.

d. You are extremely being foolish.

e. You are being foolish extremely.

In these places, it is not clear that the adverb describes the adjective. You can't write the sentence in any of these ways.

Check your answers on page 137. In examples 1 and 2, we were able to move the adverb to several different places and still be very clear. We could not, however, put an adverb between a verb and its direct object. Even one, single adverb in that position made the sentence hard to read. It made it hard to make the right connection between the verb and the direct object.

When you add more than one adverb, you may also need to avoid putting the adverbs between the subject and the verb.

The door slowly and noiselessly opened.
BETTER: The door opened slowly and noiselessly.

She slowly, carefully, and thoughtfully dialed the number.
BETTER: She dialed the number slowly, carefully, and thoughtfully.

When you add more than two adverbs, you must also add commas to separate one adverb from another. You also use a comma when you place an adverb in front of the whole sentence. This comma tells your readers that the adverb is not part of a description of the subject. Compare the difference between these two sentences.

Suddenly, the door opened.
Completely bald men save money on haircuts.

In the first sentence, the comma tells readers that the adverb is not part of the subject. In the second sentence, the adverb completely describes the adjective bald, which describes the subject noun men. By not using a comma, you tell readers that the adverb is part of the subject.

In Your Own Words

Add adverbs in the following sentences. Then rewrite each sentence by putting the same adverb in a different place.

Example: She touched the computer keys.
She lightly touched the computer keys.
or *She touched the computer keys lightly.*

1. She searched for her keys.

____

or ______________________________

2. We ate breakfast.

____

or ______________________________

3. He slammed the door.

    ____

    or ____

Compare your sentences with those on page 137.

As you saw in examples 3 and 4 on pages 90–91, some adverbs can only be placed in one spot in a sentence:

I can almost see you. You are being extremely foolish.

The meanings of the underlined adverbs will be completely lost if they are not placed right in front of the words they describe. With adverbs like these, the meaning you want an adverb to give a sentence will tell you where to put it.

Sometimes, the meaning you want to get will make a big difference in where you put an adverb. This is especially true of adverbs that can also be used as adjectives.

Try It Out

Fill in the blanks in the explanations of the following groups of sentences. The first one is done for you.

1. I just gave the waiter two dollars.
    The adverb just describes ___*when*___ the action of the verb ___*gave*___ happened. So it comes right before the verb.

    I gave just the waiter two dollars.
    The adjective just tells you it was just ___*the waiter*___. So it comes in front of that noun.

    I gave the waiter just two dollars.
    The adjective just tells you more about the quantity of ___*dollars*___. So it is placed as closely as possible to that noun.

2. We only touched that machine.

    The adverb only tells you more about the action of the verb ______________. It tells you that the people did this action and no other action. So it comes right before the verb.

We touched only that machine.

The adjective only tells you that it was only ______________ ___________ and no other. So it is placed as closely as possible to that noun.

3. She almost brought all of her children.

The adverb almost tells you more about the action of the verb ________________. She (**did, didn't**) ________________ bring children. The adverb comes in front of the verb.

She brought almost all of her children.

The adjective almost tells you more about the quantity of ________________. She (**did, didn't**) ________________ bring children. The adjective comes in front of the word all.

Check your answers on page 137.

In Your Own Words

Rewrite the following sentences. Add the words given in parentheses. Rewrite the sentence again with the same word, but move it to a different place to get a different meaning.

Example: We missed everyone. (add nearly)
We nearly missed everyone.
We missed nearly everyone.

1. We asked the clerk for one bag. (add just)

____

____

2. I did what you told me to do. (add only)

____

____

3. They stole all my money. (add almost)

Check your answers on page 137.

Put It in Writing

Go back to the photo at the start of this chapter.

1. What are the different people doing?
2. What kind of mood are they in?
3. What kind of place are they in?

Write at least three sentences. Add an adjective to every noun. Add an adverb to every verb. Then, for good measure, add an adverb to each adjective, if it makes your meaning even clearer.

Unit 3 Mastery Review

In this Unit you have seen ways to enrich your writing. You have used adjectives and adverbs for more interesting and accurate descriptions. Now, see how well you have mastered the ideas in this Unit.

Show What You Know

Use some of the words from the following list to fill in the blanks. Do not use any word more than once. Write each word in the correct form, as an adjective or as an adverb. You can also use an adverb and an adjective together. After you have filled in all the blanks, write two or three sentences of your own, to finish the story the way you would do it.

hot	perfect	excited	happy	favorite
beautiful	cold	ordinary	calm	anxious
slight	dark	amused	good	bright

[1]The good old sun was shining ________________ . [2]The radio said we had ourselves a ________________ beach day. [3]So, can you blame me if I rushed around ________________ ? [4]By eight o'clock, everyone had a bundle to carry, and we trooped off ________________ to the bus stop. [5]James had the radio on to his ________________ station. [6]Just as I saw the bus coming, I heard the radio announcer saying there was a ________________ chance of showers. [7]And all at once, the ________________ sky started getting ________________ , and I felt a ________________ drop of rain on my nose!

Compare your answers with those on page 138.

Put It In Writing

Now, take another look at the photos at the start of this Unit. Use the key words you chose back there and write an accurate and interesting description of each of the photos.

Use at least one adverb to describe the action of the soccer player. Use at least one adjective to describe the studio of the painter. And use at least one adverb and one adjective to describe the shopper in the supermarket. Of course, you can use as many adverbs and adjectives as you like in all three sentences.

Then write a fourth sentence on something you see or hear right now. Or write on something you remember so well that it seems to be happening right now. Choose your nouns and verbs well in this one!

Photo 1: ______________________________

Photo 2: ______________________________

Photo 3: ______________________________

I Can See or Hear It Now: ______________________________

UNIT 4

Showing Special Relationships

So far in this book, you have seen three reasons for writing—to tell a story, to persuade, and to describe. A fourth reason for writing is to inform, to give information without opinion.

For instance, you could give a friend directions on how to get to your house. You could describe the procedures at work for a new employee. Or you could jot down the steps in your favorite recipe. This type of writing is called informative.

If you go to a bookstore you'll find many examples of informative writing. You'll see lots of "how-to" books—from how to lose weight to how to fix a car to how to speak Spanish. These books inform: They present facts and give answers to the five W's—Who, What, Where, When, and Why—along with How.

Before You Begin

Put an X in the box next to the answer that best completes the sentence.

Informative writing is chiefly used

- ☐ a. to teach, telling facts without giving an opinion.
- ☐ b. to tell the events in a story as you remember them.
- ☐ c. to display a person or thing by picking out the most important details.
- ☐ d. to make the reader agree with your opinion.

If you put an X in the box next to a, you understand the purpose of informative writing: The writer gives information to the reader.

Of course, most writing is not only informative or only narrative or only descriptive or only persuasive. You may want to tell a story that also teaches something. Or you may give your opinion as well as the facts about a subject. Or you may describe something so that you can teach the reader something about it. After you have mastered informative writing, you will be ready to use all four types of writing and to mix the types when you need them.

Brainstorming

The photos at the start of this Unit have something in common. Each shows something that could be a topic for informative writing. As in Units 1, 2, and 3, take a good look at the photos and then write down at least one key word that could be used in an informative sentence or two about each photo. Then write down a key word or two that could be used in a couple of informative sentences on a topic of your own choosing. As before, you will use these key words when you have mastered the lessons in Chapters 9 and 10.

Photo 1: ______________________________

Photo 2: ______________________________

Photo 3: ______________________________

Here's Something I Know About: ______________________

CHAPTER 8

Writing about the Past and Future—Special Cases

Street signs and traffic signals give a lot of information that has to be understood. Could you explain to your nephew in grade school the meaning of the five signs and the WALK/DON'T WALK signal in this photo ?

There are three special tenses that help you show some complex ideas about time. These tenses are called the **perfect tenses.** All of them use a form of have as a helping verb together with the past participle of the main verb. (The past participle is one of the four principal parts we showed you in the chart on page 9.)

Try It Out

Fill in the blanks in the explanations of the examples.

Present Perfect Tense
(has or have + past participle)

1. Can show that an action was recently completed.
   Example: I have just eaten.
   Explanation: The form eaten is the past *participile* of the verb eat. This action took place in the (**distant, recent**) *recent* past.
2. Can show that an action took place at an unknown time in the past.
   Example: He has seen this show.
   Explanation: The form seen is the past ________________ of the verb see. We (**know, don't know**) ________________ exactly when this happened.
3. Can show that an action that was true in the past has continued right up to the present.
   Example: She has never driven a car.
   Explanation: The form driven is the past ________________ of the verb drive. This sentence (**is, isn't**) ________________ true of the person's past, and it is (**still, no longer**) ________________ true.

Past Perfect Tense
(had + past participle)

4. Tells that one action took place in the past before another past action.

Example: She had done the dishes before she went to bed.

Explanation: The form done is the past ________________ of the verb do. The action of doing the dishes took place **(before, after)** ________ the action of going to bed. But both actions are in the ______________.

Future Perfect Tense
(will have + past participle)

5. Tells that one action will take place in the future before another future action.

Example: I will have gone home by the time you get to the party.

Explanation: The form gone is the past ________________ of the verb go. The action of going home will take place **(before, after)** ________________ the action of someone's getting to the party. But both actions are in the ________________.

Check your answers on page 138.

LESSON 20: Present Perfect Tense

The present perfect tense describes an action that took place at some point in the past. You use the present tense forms has or have with the past participle of the main verb. This tense will give you a slightly different meaning than you can get with the simple past.

Try It Out

Change each of these three sentences from the simple past to the present perfect. First, fill in has or have and check for subject-and-verb agreement. Then fill in the past participle of the main verb. Make sure you use the past participle and not the simple past form of the main verb.

After you complete the sentences, fill in the blanks in the explanations of the new sentences.

Simple Past	Past Perfect
Example: We did the work.	We *have done* the work. The sentence now sounds as though the action happened (**recently, long ago**) *recently*.
1. You made a mistake.	You ________________ a mistake. The sentence now sounds as though the action happened (**recently, long ago**) ________________.
2. I saw him yesterday.	I ________________ him somewhere before. The sentence now sounds as though the writer (**knows, doesn't know**) ________________ when the action happened.
3. She knew what she wanted.	She ________________ always ________________ what she wanted. The sentence now sounds as though the woman's action was true in the past and is (**still true, no longer true**) ________________ of the present.

In the present perfect, sentence 1 becomes: You have made a mistake. The form have agrees with the subject you. And the form made is the past participle of the verb make.

In both the example and sentence 1, the simple past tells you a simple fact about something the person did in the past. By changing to the present perfect, you create a feeling that the action just happened, only a moment ago. The use of have emphasizes how recently in the past the action took place. The meanings of these sentences are very close. The simple past is not wrong. The present perfect just adds emphasis.

In the present perfect, sentence 2 becomes: I have seen him somewhere before. The form have agree with the subject I. The form seen is the past participle of see.

There is a difference in meaning between this second pair of sentences. "I saw him yesterday" tells you about a definite time in the past. The exact time is not so clear in "I have seen him somewhere before." The present perfect emphasizes the fact that the writer is not sure when a past action took place.

In the present perfect, sentence 3 becomes: She has always known what she wanted. The form has agrees with the singular subject she. The form known is the past participle of the verb know.

Try It Out

Read the following sentences. In the second sentence of each group, if you would use the simple past, put an X in the box under **Simple Past** in front of the sentence. If you would use the present perfect tense, put an X in the box under **Present Perfect** in front of the sentence. Then cross out the verb form in parentheses that you did not choose.

Simple Past	**Present Perfect**	
☐	☐	1. Today, you left a job that you held for two years. I (**worked**) (**have worked**) there for two years.
☐	☐	2. Two years ago, you started working for your aunt. I (**worked**) (**have worked**) for her for two years now.
☐	☐	3. Your friend is now taking a course in computers. She (**wanted**) (**has wanted**) to get a better job.
☐	☐	4. Tonight, your friend said she would skip dessert. She (**did not want**) (**has not wanted**) to gain any more weight.
☐	☐	5. Your friend has a test tomorrow, and he still plans to read for another half hour. He (**studied**) (**has studied**) for hours already.
☐	☐	6. Your friend bought new snow tires. He (**needed**) (**has needed**) snow tires.

Sentences 1, 4, and 6 talk about something that is finished, so the simple past can be used. In sentences 2, 3, and 5, the action has continued from the past to the present, so the present perfect tense is used.

When you use the present perfect tense, you may want to use a contraction of the subject and the verbs has or have. A contraction is a way of writing two words together with an apostrophe ('). But don't forget what the contraction means:

I've = I have	you've = you have
he's = he has	we've = we have
she's = she has	they've = they have
it's = it has	

Try It Out

Fill in the blanks with the correct form of the main verb. Then rewrite the sentence without a contraction.

Example: That coat's seen better days. **(see)**
MEANS: That coat has seen better days.

1. You've ____________ my favorite chair. **(break)**

   MEANS: ______________________________

2. She's ____________ you already. **(forgive)**

   MEANS: ______________________________

3. We've ____________ you how to do this. **(teach)**

   MEANS: ______________________________

4. It's ____________ me six years to save that money. **(take)**

   MEANS: ______________________________

5. They've ____________ to class every day this week. **(be)**

   MEANS: ______________________________

In these sentences, you've broken means you have broken; she's forgiven means she has forgiven; we've taught means we have taught; and it's taken means it has taken; and they've been means they have been.

In Your Own Words

Write three sentences of your own using the present perfect tense. You can use contractions if you like.

1. Think of something that happened to someone you know in the past. Now, imagine that it has just happened a few seconds ago. Tell what has just happened. Use the word just in your sentence.

   ____

2. Think of something you and a friend have done together at some time in the past. Tell about it as though you can't remember exactly when you did it.

   ____

3. Think of something that someone you know has always done in the past and still does now. Use the word always in your sentence.

   ____

Compare your sentences with those on page 138.

LESSON 21: Past Perfect Tense

The past perfect tense can help you emphasize that one of two past actions happened before the other. You use had, the past tense form of have, together with the past participle of the main verb.

Try It Out

First, fill in the helping verb had. Then fill in the past participle of the verb given in parentheses at the end of the sentence.

After you complete the sentences, fill in the blanks in the explanation of the sentences.

1. He ______________ me a raise last month, but he gave me another one today. **(give)**
2. After we ______________ all the coffee, we drank tea. **(drink)**
3. They ______________ just ______________ dinner when the fire began. **(begin)**

In these sentences, both actions took place in the ____________.

The action in the first part of the sentence took place ____________

the action in the second part.

The first action in each of these sentences took place before the second action. Yet the second action also took place in the past. The past perfect tense shows that the first action happened before the second action:

First: He had given me a raise last month.
Second: He gave me another one today.

First: We had drunk all the coffee.
Second: We drank tea.

First: They had just begun dinner.
Second: The fire began.

In the first two sentences, you could use the simple past for all the verbs: He gave me a raise last month, but he gave me another one today. After we drank all the coffee, we drank tea. The other words in these sentences already tell the reader the order in which the actions took place. The words last month and today in the first sentence tell you the order. The word after in the second sentence also tells you the order of the actions. The use of the past perfect simply emphasizes the order.

The third sentence does not seem as clear when both verbs are in the simple past: They just began dinner when the fire began. The use of the past perfect helps the writer avoid confusing the reader with two verbs that are exactly the same.

Try It Out

As you have seen, you can use both the simple past and the past perfect tenses together in a sentence to show the order of events that occurred in the past. Read the following sentences. Use either the past or past perfect form of the verb in parentheses to make the sentence clear.

Example: I *had left* **(leave)** for work before the snow *started* **(start).**

1. When I ________________ **(finish)** my housework for the day, I ________________ television.

2. As Marcus __________ **(enter)** the room, he knew he __________ **(be)** there before.

3. They __________ **(arrive)** at the station after the train __________ **(pull)** away.

4. The tour guide __________ **(mention)** places that we __________ **(see)** already.

5. She __________ **(begin)** to realize what her friend David __________ **(do).**

Check your answers on page 138.

In Your Own Words

Try to write three sentences using past and past perfect tenses. First, give the actions, in order. Then combine the actions in a sentence. You may need to use such time words as before, after, when, just.

Example: First: *I had started my diet*
Second: *I lost ten pounds*
I lost ten pounds after I had started my diet.

1. First: __________
   Second: __________
   ____

2. First: __________
   Second: __________
   ____

3. First: __________
   Second: __________
   ____

Compare your sentences with those on page 138.

When you write sentences in the past perfect tense, you can use a contraction of the verb had:

I'd = I had
he'd = he had
she'd = he had
you'd = you had
we'd = we had
they'd = they had

Try It Out

Fill in the blanks with the correct form of the main verb. Then rewrite the sentence without a contraction.

Example: We'd *eaten* so much, we just fell asleep. **(eat)**
MEANS: *We had eaten so much, we just fell asleep.*

1. After I'd __________ her six times, she finally understood. **(tell)**

   MEANS: ______________________________

2. She'd __________ it a secret, but we all knew anyway. **(keep)**

   MEANS: ______________________________

3. The bomb didn't go off because he'd __________ the wrong fuse. **(light)**

   MEANS: ______________________________

4. After you'd __________, they showed their home movies. **(leave)**

   MEANS: ______________________________

5. They'd __________ only four hours when the alarm rang. **(sleep)**

   MEANS: ______________________________

In these sentences, I'd told means I had told; she'd kept means she had kept; he'd lit means he had lit; you'd left means you had left; and they'd slept means they had slept.

In Your Own Words

Write three sentences of your own using the past perfect tense.

1. Tell about two things you did today. Write a sentence to tell which thing you did first. Use the following pattern:

   After I (first action) at (time), I (second action).

   Example: After *I had taken* the dog for a walk at *6:00 this morning,* I *ran* to catch my bus.

   ____

   ____

2. Tell about two things someone you know did last weekend. Write a sentence to tell which thing the person did first. Use the following pattern:

   Before (name) (second action), he/she (first action).

   Example: Before *Joe showed up* at my party, he *had* already *eaten* dinner at Marge's.

   ____

   ____

3. Tell us about two things you and someone else have done together in the past. Write a sentence to tell us which thing you did first. You can use either the before or after patterns we've shown you.

   ____

   ____

Compare your sentences with those on page 138.

LESSON 22: Future Perfect Tense

The future perfect tense helps you compare two points in time in the future. You can show that one future action will take place at a time before another future action. You use will have—the future tense of have—with the past participle of the main verb.

Try It Out

Fill in the blanks in the following sentences. First, fill in the helping verb will have. Then fill in the past participle of the verb given in parentheses. Make sure you use the past participle and not the simple past form of the main verb.

After you complete each sentence, fill in the blanks in the explanations of the sentences. The first one has been done for you.

1. John *will have left* by the time Red gets here. **(leave)**
   Red will get here at a time in the *future*. By that time, someone could talk about John's leaving as also having happened in the *future*.

2. I ________________ twenty pounds by this time next month. **(lose)**
   Next month is in the ________________. By that time, someone could talk about the action of losing weight as also having happened in the ________________.

3. If I drink another cup, I ________________ ten cups of coffee today. **(have)**
   The action of drinking another cup might take place in the ________________. If and when that happens, someone could talk about the action of drinking ten cups as also having happened in the ________________.

In sentence 1, both John's action and Red's will take place in the future. But John's action will happen first. John's action will be in the past by the time Red's action takes place. This relationship in time is shown by using the future perfect tense—will have left—for John's action. Red's future action is shown with the present-tense form gets.

In sentence 2, the action of losing weight will be completed (and therefore will be in the past) by a stated point in time in the future. This is shown by using the future perfect tense—will have lost. By the time I have lost twenty pounds, next month will be in my past.

In sentence 3, the future perfect tense—will have had—shows the reader that something, such as drinking too much coffee, might be accomplished in the future.

Try It Out

As you have seen, you can use both the present and the future perfect tenses together in a sentence to show the order of events that will occur in the future. Read the following sentences. Use either the present or future perfect form of the verb in parentheses to make the sentence clear.

Example: Before the program *is* **(be)** over, *we will have seen* **(see)** eight commercials.

1. By the time Carl ____________________ **(read)** his book, I ____________________ **(read)** three.
2. They ____________________ **(finish)** dinner by the time we ____________________ **(get)** there.
3. If I ____________________ **(eat)** another cookie, I ____________________ **(eat,** the entire box.
4. Before he ____________________ **(see)** me, I ____________________ **(get)** my hair permed.
5. When she ____________________ **(call)** tomorrow, I ____________________ **(make)** a decision about whom to hire.

Check your answers on page 139.

In Your Own Words

Complete the following sentences using the present or the future perfect tense where appropriate. The answers are your choice of words.

Example: Before the day is over, I will have finished this sweater.

1. By the time you see me, ____________________.
2. If ____________________, you will look like a blimp.
3. ____________________ by next week.
4. Unless ____________________, I will feel too tired tomorrow.
5. ____________________ before we get there.

Compare your sentences with those on page 139.

Just as you can use contractions of have with the present perfect tense, and contractions of had with the past perfect tense, you can use contractions of will have with the future perfect tense. These are the contractions for subject pronouns with the helping word will:

I'll	= I will	you'll	= you will
he'll	= he will	she'll	= she will
we'll	= we will	they'll	= they will

Note that when you use the future perfect with not, you use the contraction won't for will not:

I'll have studied. = I will have studied.
I won't have studied. = I will not have studied.

Try It Out

Fill in the blank spaces in the following sentences, using the future perfect tense. Then re-write the sentence on the line given, not using contractions.

Example: He'll have *finished* studying when you call him. **(finish)**
MEANS: *He will have finished studying when you call him.*

1. You'll have ______________ a dozen eggs by the time you've finished making breakfast for this family. **(break)**

   MEANS: ______________________________

   ____

2. I won't have ______________ halfway there when the party's already started. **(get)**

   MEANS: ______________________________

   ____

3. She'll have ______________ asleep before we get there. **(fall)**

MEANS: ____________________

____

4. They'll have ____________ to every senator in Congress before the night is over. **(write)**

MEANS: ____________________

____

5. He'll have ____________ with the sunrise. **(go)**

MEANS: ____________________

In these sentences, you'll have broken means you will have broken; I won't have gotten means I will not have gotten; she'll have fallen means she will have fallen; they'll have written means they will have written; and he'll have gone means he will have gone.

In Your Own Words

1. Think about two things you will do tomorrow. Tell about both things in the same sentence. Tell which will have been completed by the time the other happens.

   Example: By the time I *get to work*, I *will have heard the news*.

   ____

2. Write the same kind of sentence again. This time, tell about another person you know.

   ____

3. Think about something you or someone you know plans to have done by some date in the future.

   Suggestions: By next New Year's Day, I ____________

   By my next birthday, I ____________

   ____

Compare your sentences with those on page 139.

Reminder

The simple past form and the past participle of many irregular verbs are not the same. The simple past form is only used in the past tense. All perfect tenses require the past participle.

Wrong: You have ate my lunch.
Right: You have eaten my lunch.

Wrong: He had took the wrong bus.
Right: He had taken the wrong bus.

Wrong: We had did what you wanted.
Right: We had done what you wanted.

Check Your Skills: Use the Present Perfect Tense

Use the **present perfect tense** to complete the following sentences. Use the verb given in parentheses at the end of each sentence. Check for correct subject-and-verb agreement with has or have. Check to make sure you are using the past participle of the main verb.

1. That plant ________________ two inches since yesterday. **(grow)**
2. You ________________ just ________________ the last cookie. **(eat)**
3. The weather ________________ colder in the last few days. **(get)**
4. I think she ________________ you before. **(meet)**
5. They ________________ never ________________ their children alone. **(leave)**

Now, rewrite each of these five sentences using contractions.

6. ____.
7. ____.
8. ____.

9. ____.

10. ____.

Check your answers on page 139.

Check Your Skills: Use the Past Perfect Tense

Use the **past perfect tense** to complete the following sentences. Use the verb given in parentheses at the end of each sentence. Check to make sure you are using the past participle of the main verb.

1. We ________________ that car for six years before it needed any repairs. **(drive)**
2. After he ________________ the first three miles of the race, he decided to quit. **(run)**
3. They ________________ about it for weeks, but they only told me about it yesterday. **(know)**
4. I ________________ ten pictures before I realized that there was no film in the camera. **(take)**
5. The phone ________________ ten times before he finally answered it. **(ring)**

Now rewrite the first four sentences using contractions.

6. ____.
7. ____.
8. ____.
9. ____.

Check your answers on page 139.

Check Your Skills: Use the Future Perfect Tense

Use the **future perfect tense** to complete the following sentences. Use the verb given in parentheses at the end of the sentence.

1. If you lose again, I ______________________ you six times in a row. **(beat)**
2. I'm sure he ______________________ already before he comes home. **(eat)**
3. By the time we get there, the movie ______________________. **(begin)**

Check your answers on page 139.

Check Your Skills: Write about Actions with the Perfect Tenses

Use one of the perfect tenses to complete the following sentences. Use the verb given in parentheses at the end of each sentence. Check for correct subject-and-verb agreement. Also check to see that you are using the past participle of the main verb.

Then explain why you used the tense. Circle the letter of the correct reason.

1. Gary ______________ just ______________ out his last pair of jeans. **(wear)**
   a. A recently completed action
   b. An action that was true in the past and has continued right up to the present
   c. An action that will take place in the future before another future action

2. The pilot admitted that he ____________ never ____________ that kind of plane before. **(fly)**
   a. A recently completed action
   b. An action that took place in the past before another past action
   c. An action that will take place in the future before another future action

3. I ________________ never ________________ in an airplane, have you? **(be)**
   a. A recently completed action
   b. An action that was true in the past and has continued right up to the present
   c. An action that took place in the past before another past action

4. By the time you see us, we ________________ a new car. **(buy)**
   a. A recently completed action
   b. An action that took place in the past before another past action
   c. An action that will take place in the future before another future action

5. I painted over the things my kids ________________ on the bedroom walls. **(draw)**
   a. An action that was true in the past and has continued right up to the present
   b. An action that took place in the past before another past action
   c. An action that will take place in the future before another future action

6. Lucy ________________ she wasn't going, but she changed her mind. **(say)**
   a. A recently completed action
   b. An action that was true in the past and that has continued right up to the present
   c. An action that took place in the past before another past action

7. Art ________________ the bill now, so we can leave. **(pay)**
   a. A recently completed action
   b. An action that was true in the past and has continued right up to the present
   c. An action that took place at a time in the past, but the exact time is not known

8. I'm sure your dog ________________ home by the time we get back to your place. **(come)**
   a. A recently completed action
   b. An action that took place in the past before another past action
   c. An action that will take place in the future before another future action

Check your answers on page 139.

Put It in Writing

Go back to the start of this chapter. Five signs are shown in the photo:

ONE WAY

DON'T EVEN THINK OF PARKING HERE

BUS STOP/NO STANDING

RED ZONE/TOW & FINE $100 MINIMUM

BUSES ONLY

There is also a WALK/DON'T WALK signal. In complete sentences, explain the meaning of these signs. Give the reason for each of them. You can make up a meaning and a reason. Use the present perfect, the past perfect, and the future perfect tenses when you give the reasons that the city puts up these signs.

Unit 4 Mastery Review

In this Unit you have practiced writing sentences in the past perfect, present perfect, and future perfect tenses. You have seen how to write about two different actions in the past, showing which action took place before the other. You have also seen how to write about the future, showing which of two actions will take place before the other.

You have also practiced writing sentences in the passive voice, when the subject of the sentence is not doing the action.

Show What You Know

Use words from the following list to fill in the blanks in this recipe. Be careful about verb tenses. Try to use only the perfect tenses. Do not use any verb helpers like <u>could</u>, <u>should</u>, or <u>must</u>.

fill	pick	bubble	add
sit	boil	wonder	make

[1]If you ______________ ever ______________ water, you can make perfect hard-cooked eggs. [2]After you ______________ two or three eggs, you'll check that their shells have no cracks. [3]You ______________ also already ______________ a saucepan with enough cold water to cover the eggs with an inch of water. [4]You ______________ a teaspoon of salt to the water, too, to help harden the shells. When everything is ready, you'll use a medium-high flame to bring the water to a boil. [5]When the water ______________ for a minute, you'll cover the pan and turn off the heat. [6]After the eggs ______________ for fifteen to twenty minutes, you'll pour the very hot water out of the pan and

run cold water over the warm eggs. [7]And that's all there is to it! You ________________ perfect hard-cooked eggs with smooth uncracked shells. [8]I myself ________________ for years how the trick was done, and I was amazed to learn how easy it actually was!

Check your answers on page 140.

Put It in Writing

You have now completed all the lessons in this book. Before you attempt your final mastery exercises, take another look at the photos that started this Unit. Each shows something that can be explained.

- Write at least one sentence in the past perfect tense for photo 1.
- Write at least one sentence in the present perfect tense for photo 2.
- Write at least one sentence in the future perfect tense for photo 3.

After you have written about the photos, take another look at the last group of key words at the start of this Unit. Use at least some of these words to teach a reader something that you yourself know very well.

Photo 1: ____

____

Photo 2: ____

____

Photo 3: ____

____

Here's What I Know: ________________________________

____

Final Mastery Test

Section 1

There are 50 items in this section of the test. The test asks you to use the skills you have studied in this book. After you have completed the test, use the chart on page 128 to decide which parts of this book you should review before going on to the other books in this series: IMPROVING SENTENCES and USING PARAGRAPHS.

Verb Tenses and Subject-and-Verb Agreement

Fill in the blanks in the following sentences with a form of the verb given in parentheses at the end of each sentence. Choose the tenses that correctly show the meanings of the sentences and that fit into the blank lines. Then check for subject-and-verb agreement.

1. Everyone ____________________ someone to love, and that includes you! **(need)**
2. Here ____________________ the keys to my car. **(be)**
3. I'm glad I wasn't paying for dinner last night. Ten dollars ____________________ all I had on me. **(be)**
4. My new jeans ____________________ so tight I could barely move. **(be)**
5. ____________________ you going to ____________________ the day off tomorrow? **(take)**
6. They ____________________ about to ____________________ for the loan when they noticed the high interest rate. **(sign)**

7. She ________________ always ________________ about dying, and it makes me nervous. (**talk**)
8. At this very moment, his two sons and his daughter ________________ ________________ a big party for his birthday next week. (**plan**)
9. One of my friends at work ________________ ________________ a cup of coffee when the fire alarm went off. (**get**)
10. You ________________ ________________ yourself so much last night that I hated to ask you to leave. (**enjoy**)
11. Don't call me before 10:00 tomorrow. I ________________ ________________ ________________ late. (**sleep**)
12. We can't come to your house next Saturday. We ________________ ________________ ________________ the game on television. (**watch**)
13. He says he ________________ ________________ to his diet, but somebody's eating a lot of cookies! (**keep**)
14. The schedule says her bus ________________ ________________ in five minutes, so I hope she's on her way to the terminal. (**arrive**)
15. My boss ________________ always ________________ me to try. (**encourage**)
16. He ________________ ________________ an answer for you tomorrow, but I wouldn't bet on it. (helper + **have**)
17. You've been bicycling for two hours now. Look at how you're sweating! You ________________ ________________ tired. (helper + **be**)

18. You ________________ ________________ more vegetables and less sugar. (helper for good habit + **eat**)

19. I really ________________ ________________ your cooking. I'm just not hungry right now. (helper + **like**)

20. You ________________ ________________ your car! I thought you were only joking. (helper + **sell**)

21. They ________________ ________________ the park for the celebration after all. (**clean** + helper for emphasis)

22. Someone ________________ just ________________ away in your car. (**drive**)

23. Neither my co-workers nor my boss ________________ ________________ him since last Friday. (**see**)

24. I ________________ ________________ this show for years. (**watch**)

25. I ________________ ________________ never to tell anyone, but I had to tell you. (**swear**)

26. My family ________________ ________________ in that apartment before buying a house. (**live**)

27. Before he cooked the dinner, he ________________ ________________ the oven. (**clean**)

28. Tina ________________ ________________ ________________ by the time you get here. (**leave**)

29. Next Saturday, I ________________ ________________ ________________ in this country for ten years. (**be**)

30. After I paint this room, I ________________ ________________ ________________ the whole house. (**paint**)

Pronouns

Fill in the blanks in the following sentences with one of the following pronouns: I, me, he, him, she, her, we, us, they, them.

31. I may as well lie. No one believes ______________ anyway.
32. I start working for Ms. Johnson tomorrow. What kind of boss is ______________?
33. They're laying off three other workers besides me. The boss called ______________ into the office this morning.
34. Why don't you two ride with me? ______________ three can easily fit in my car.
35. I'm inviting the Warner twins. I'll give ______________ the details tomorrow.
36. I hear the Garcias aren't speaking to you and Linda. I hope that taught you and ______________ a lesson about getting involved in other people's problems.
37. Just between you and ______________, don't tell Carla that I know about this. She thinks it's a secret.
38. I was sorry to hear that Frank is leaving town. It won't be the same here without ______________.

Adjectives and Adverbs

Fill in the blanks with the correct form of the word given at the end of the sentence.

39. I ______________ asked for a black tie. **(specific)**
40. This punch smells ______________. **(sweet)**
41. I feel ______________ about what I said. **(unhappy)**

42. You sound so ________________ . Why don't you take a nap? **(tired)**

43. My forehead is hot and I don't feel so ________________ . **(good)**

44. I like the song you wrote, but my nephew thinks it sounds ________________ . **(loud)**

45. The children were playing so ________________ I couldn't hear myself think. **(noisy)**

46. They were running so ________________ I couldn't catch up to them. **(quick)**

47. The children are being too ________________ . They're up to some mischief. **(quiet)**

48. You must want this raise ________________ ________________ . **(awful + bad)**

49. If you do this job ________________ ________________ , you'll find a bonus in your envelope on payday. **(real + good)**

50. He shouted so ________________ , you could hear him from across the street. **(loud)**

END OF SECTION 1. Answers are on page 140.

SECTION 2

Read the following sentences. Each gives you a topic for sentences that **narrate, describe, persuade,** or **inform.** Write at least three sentences for each of the topics.

Topic 1. Tell about three things you've seen or done since you woke up today.

Topic 2. Describe three dishes you had for dinner last night. Include the colors and tastes of each food.

Topic 3. A child asks you what a library does. Can you point out three services that a library has to offer?

Topic 4. The party's over, and your friend has had one drink too many. Give him or her three good reasons to let you do the driving tonight.

CHECKLIST

	Yes	No
1. Did I use the best and the correct verb tense?	☐	☐
2. Did I make every verb agree with the subject of its sentence?	☐	☐
3. Did I write every pronoun in the correct subject or object form?	☐	☐
4. Did I use adjectives and adverbs to make my meaning clear and lively?	☐	☐
5. Did I try to use narration, persuasion, description, and information to help the reader understand?	☐	☐

END OF FINAL MASTERY TEST

If You Missed the Following:	You Should Review			
	Unit	Chapter	Lesson	On Pages:
VERB TENSES				
1 2 3 4 5 6	1	1	3	11–16
7 8 9 10 11 12	1	2	4	20–23
13 14 15	1	2	5	23–24
16 17 18	1	3	6	29–31
19 20 21	1	3	7	32–33
22 23 24	4	8	20	103–107
25 26 27	4	8	21	107–111
28 29 30	4	8	22	111–116
SUBJECT-AND-VERB AGREEMENT				
2 3 4	2	4	8	42–45
8 9	2	4	10	47–49
1 19 22	2	4	11	50–53
PRONOUNS				
31 32 33 34	2	5	12	58–60
35 36	2	5	13	60–61
37 38	2	5	14	62–63
ADJECTIVES AND ADVERBS				
39 40 41 42 43 44	3	6	15	73–77
45 46 47	3	6	16	78–80
48 49 50	3	6	17	80–82

ANSWERS

UNIT 1 Showing Time when You Write

CHAPTER 1 Writing about the Past, Present, and Future

LESSON 1: Showing Time in Your Sentences

In Your Own Words

1. I used to live with my parents.
2. I work from 9 to 5.
3. I will be promoted in May.

LESSON 2: The Building Blocks of the System of Tenses

Try It Out

1. applied	2. carried	3. dried
4. obeyed	5. destroyed	6. denied
7. arguing	8. dating	9. choosing
10. smoking	11. lying	12. tying
13. begged	14. fanning	15. dropped
16. fixing	17. slipped	18. training
19. preferring	20. occurred	

In Your Own Words

This morning I learned that my pickup was broken. I was planning to get a new starter, but I had forgotten. I had no way to get to work. I decided to walk. My brother had given me a Walkman for Christmas. So I brought it with me. I listened to music as I hurried along. I got so interested in my music, I walked right past the building where I work. Luckily for me, the tape ended, or I might have walked right to another city!

LESSON 3: Writing with the Present, Past, and Future Tenses

A. Present Tense

In Your Own Words

1. Patty smokes one pack of cigarettes every day.
2. The sun always sets in the west.
3. Class starts at 3:00 this afternoon.

B. Past Tense

In Your Own Words

1. I went to the beach yesterday.
2. I played baseball when I was a child.
3. I brushed my teeth this morning.

C. Future Tenses

In Your Own Words

1. I will go to the dentist tomorrow.
2. Eve is going to get married in June.
3. They are about to leave the room.

Check Your Skills: Write about Actions in the Past, Present, and Future

1. wrote
2. spoke
3. burst
4. grew
5. blew
6. caught
7. built
8. bet
9. came
10. beat
11. boils
12. sells
13. carries
14. teaches
15. tries
16. am going to see
17. is going to quit
18. are going to like
19. is about to sing
20. are about to say

Check Your Skills: Change the Time of Actions in a Paragraph

Last week, I went to the store. I bought things for your birthday. While I was there, I got a new tube of toothpaste. I also chose a tube of fancy icing for your cake.

CHAPTER 2 Writing about Continuous Actions

LESSON 4: Using the Progressive Tenses

A. The Present Progressive

In Your Own Words

1. I am writing a sentence.
2. He is reading a book.
3. They are watching television.

B. The Past Progressive

In Your Own Words

1. I was working in the garden for several hours yesterday.
2. Marge was playing tennis for several hours before I arrived.
3. They were waiting several hours in line before they finally got their tickets.

C. The Future Progressive

In Your Own Words

1. I will be using the telephone for several hours tomorrow.
2. Anita will be shopping at the mall for several hours tomorrow.
3. We will be going to the park for several hours tomorrow afternoon.

LESSON 5: Special Uses of the Present Progressive

In Your Own Words

1. My best friend will be arriving next weekend.
2. We are going tonight.
3. I will be working tomorrow.

Check Your Skills: Write about Actions with Progressive Tenses

1. am winning
2. is losing
3. are studying
4. is complaining
5. are thinking
6. was taking
7. were singing
8. was planning
9. were becoming
10. were looking
11. will be sleeping
12. will be watching
13. will be waiting
14. will be seeing
15. will be transmitting

Check Your Skills: Change the Time Shown by the Verbs in a Paragraph

In our company, things are changing. Workers today are getting better pay and they are working fewer hours than ever before. Bosses are taking their workers' advice for improvements. The company is giving free day care for employees' children. It is even holding free exercise classes every day at noon.

CHAPTER 3 Writing with Other Kinds of Verb Helpers

LESSON 6: Using Helpers to Change the Meaning of a Verb

In Your Own Words

1. Everyone should be exercising every day.
2. Greg might be driving over her right now.
3. I wanted to go to the game yesterday.

LESSON 7: Using Forms of Do to Help Verbs

In Your Own Words

1. I did like that movie.
2. Does the earth revolve around the sun?
3. Do you have to smoke while I am eating?
4. No, I don't have to smoke while you are eating.

Check Your Skills: Use Verb Helpers

2. He should be working.
3. That coat must cost a fortune.
4. They may be eating dinner.
5. She would understand your reasons.

Check Your Skills: Use Forms of Do

1. He does look better without his beard.
2. I do want to go to the party.
3. That rabbit's foot does bring me good luck.
4. You do want to marry me!

5. Does he drink coffee?
6. Do her parents understand her decision?
7. Does your doctor give you sleeping pills?
8. He doesn't take things very seriously.
9. They don't know the answer.
10. My mother doesn't want to live in a nursing home.

UNIT 1 MASTERY REVIEW

Show What You Know

Last night, I was really glad I had learned first aid. Joe and I were eating at a new restaurant. "I come here all the time," said Joe. That was his big mistake: He talked with his mouth full. Joe started choking on a bone that was caught in his throat. I knew what a person should do in just such a situation. I performed the Heimlich maneuver. Joe's life was saved.

UNIT 2 MASTERY REVIEW

CHAPTER 4 Writing Verbs to Agree with Subjects

LESSON 8: Checking Agreement with the It-versus-They Test

In Your Own Words

1. One hundred miles is a long way to walk.
2. Two months isn't enough time to get the job done.
3. Three hundred pounds is too heavy for me to lift.

A. Singular Subjects that Look like Plurals

In Your Own Words

1. He started the athletics department at the school.
2. Barbara was learning electronics in her spare time.
3. The good news spread quickly through the office.

B. Singular Subjects That Take the Plural Form of the Verb

In Your Own Words

1. The scissors are not very sharp.
2. My glasses need tightening.
3. Don't you think your jeans are getting too ragged?

LESSON 9: Finding the Simple Subject to Check Agreement

In Your Own Words

1. is (singular) 2. bothers (singular) 3. were (plural)

A. Finding the Subject in Sentences Beginning with Here and There

In Your Own Words

1. What has happened to your new motorcycle?
2. When are you going to take me to dinner?
3. Here are the clothes to take to the Salvation Army.
4. There are the beans, baking in the oven.

LESSON 10: Checking Agreement with Compound Subjects

B. Subjects joined with Either . . . or, Neither . . . nor, or Not only . . . , but also

In Your Own Words

1. My mother and father are very proud of us.
2. Either pollution or cigarettes are causing that cough.
3. Neither the President nor his aides know what they are doing.
4. Religion and politics are subjects that should not be brought up at parties.
5. Not only his temper, but also his habits make him an unlikely candidate for the job.

LESSON 11: Special Problems in Subject-and-Verb Agreement

C. Subjects That Can Be Either Singular or Plural

In Your Own Words

1. Nothing in that store is of any interest to me.
2. Most of the people in the United States have ancestors who were immigrants.
3. My favorite team is playing tonight.
4. Anyone who believes in astrology is crazy.
5. Both of those sweaters look nice on you.

Check Your Skills: Check Agreement with the It-versus-They Test

1. is
2. is
3. need
4. travels
5. is
6. is
7. is
8. are

Check Your Skills:
Find Simple Subjects to Solve Subject-and-Verb Agreement

1. was
2. stands
3. is
4. are
5. were

Check Your Skills:
Check Subject-and-Verb Agreement with Compound Subjects

1. look
2. is
3. are
4. is
5. makes

Check Your Skills: Check Subjects and Verbs for Agreement

	Simple Subject	Singular or Plural	Verb
1. need	pants	P	need
2. seems	cause	S	seems
3. is	money	S	is
4. think	Fred and his mother	P	think
5. is	orchestra	S	is
6. are	books	P	are
7. has	everyone	S	has
8. cost	both	P	cost
9. are	parents	P	are
10. gives	half	S	gives
11. was	two tablespoons	S	was
12. has	United States	S	has
13. are	scissors	S	are
14. are	effects	P	are
15. do	children	P	do
16. wants	wife	S	wants
17. loses	team	S	loses
18. is	man	S	is
19. needs	somebody	S	needs
20. think	some	P	think
21. is	miles	S	is
22. is	mathematics	S	is
23. sing	The Beatles	S	sing
24. is	one	S	is
25. was	most	S	was

CHAPTER 5 Writing with Pronouns

LESSON 12: Checking for Subjects and Direct Objects

Try It Out

1. They
2. It
3. We
4. She
5. He

Try It Out

1. them
2. him
3. it
4. her
5. us

In Your Own Words

1. I like taking care of them.
2. We need more people like him in our company.

3. He helps us because he is a generous person.
4. Your attitude surprises me.
5. You have the money, so buy them.

LESSON 13: Checking for Indirect Objects

In Your Own Words

1. Someone else should give him the letter.
2. They sent me another bill.
3. I read about them in the newspaper.

LESSON 14: Checking Pronouns Used with Prepositions

In Your Own Words

1. All the attention was on them.
2. A diamond was missing from it.
3. With him on our side we can't lose.

Check Your Skills: Write the Correct Forms of Pronouns

1. I	2. me	3. I we	4. me
5. me	6. me	7. him	8. he
9. him he	10. she	11. us	12. her
13. me	14. them	15. us	16. we
17. they I us	18. them us	19. me	

UNIT 2 Writing Clear Sentences

Show What You Know

1. has	2. do	3. claims	4. fills
5. is	6. wants	7. looks	8. asks

1. I	2. her	3. she	4. I
5. him	6. he	7. them	8. they

UNIT 3 Writing Descriptive Sentences

CHAPTER 6 Descriptive Writing with Adjectives and Adverbs

Try It Out

seven strange new

Try It Out

softly yesterday always endlessly outside

LESSON 15: Telling the Difference Between Adjectives and Adverbs

2. excitedly
3. frozen
4. broken
5. bitingly
6. angrily

In Your Own Words

1. Anita carefully picked out an outfit for her interview.
2. Ken's throbbing headache made it impossible for him to finish his work.
3. Bill remained calm in spite of the floor.
4. Marsha always looks confused in Math class.
5. Ben entered the race to prove that his car is fast.
6. Margaret got out of bed and answered the phone sleepily.

LESSON 16: Using Linking Verbs and Adjectives

Try It Out

1. angry
2. angrily
3. angry
4. frantic
5. frantically
6. impatient
7. quickly
8. clam
9. suddenly
10. terrible

Try It Out

1. good
2. good
3. bad
4. badly
5. bad
6. well
7. good
8. well.

In Your Own Words

1. Beth's chicken tastes hopelessly bad.
2. Kevin sounded terribly upset on the phone.
3. A thousand dollars seems an awfully high price for fixing the roof.
4. My friends are feeling very energetic.

LESSON 17: Making Adjectives and Adverbs Stronger

Check Your Skills: Use Adjectives and Adverbs in Sentences

1. busily
2. well
3. quickly
4. quick
5. sleepily
6. sleepy
7. great
8. greatly
9. badly
10. bravely

Check Your Skills: Make Adjectives and Adverbs Stronger

1. This stew tastes <u>awfully</u> salty.
2. You seem <u>extremely</u> happy.
3. They are working <u>very</u> slowly.
4. You sang that song <u>especially</u> well.
5. The tired children were <u>unbelievably</u> patient.

CHAPTER 7 Putting Adjectives and Adverbs in the Right Place

Try It Out

2. boy bought balloon
3. parents gave children love
4. boy is baseball player
5. day was sunny

LESSON 18: Adding Adjectives

In Your Own Words

1. The crippled woman crossed the wide street.
2. The lumpy sofa looked uncomfortable.
3. The torn book lay open on the glass table.

LESSON 19: Adding Adverbs

Try It Out

2. She dialed number
   a,b,c slowly dialed
3. I can see you
   a. almost see
4. you being foolish
   a. extremely

In Your Own Words

1. She searched frantically for her keys.
   or She searched for her keys frantically.
2. We ate breakfast quickly.
   or We quickly ate breakfast.
3. He angrily slammed the door.
   or He slammed the door angrily.

Try It Out

2. touched that machine
3. brought did
4. children did

In Your Own Words

1. We just asked the clerk for one bag.
   We asked the clerk for just one bag.
2. I did only what you told me to do.
   I only did what you told me to do.
3. They almost stole all my money.
   They stole almost all my money.

UNIT 3 MASTERY REVIEW

Show What You Know

The good old sun was shining brightly. The radio said we had ourselves a perfect beach day. So, can you blame me if I rushed around excitedly? By eight o'clock, everyone had a bundle to carry, and we trooped off happily to the bus stop. James had the radio on to his favorite station. Just as I saw the bus coming, I heard the radio announcer saying there was a slight chance of showers. And all at once, the beautiful sky started getting dark, and I felt a cold drop on my nose! "Don't you dare !" James said loudly. And, sure enough, that little cloud hurried on its way, giving us only a light drizzle!

UNIT 4 Showing Special Relationships

CHAPTER 8 Writing about the Past and Future—Special Cases

Try It Out

2. participle don't know
3. participle is still
4. participle before past
5. participle before future

LESSON 20: Present Perfect Tense

In Your Own Words

1. Jesse has just been fired from his job.
2. Hope and I have gone to that beach before.
3. Donna has always acted like a spoiled child.

LESSON 21: Past Perfect Tense

Try It Out

1. had given
2. had drunk
3. had begun

Try It Out

1. had finished watched
2. entered had been
3. arrived had pulled
4. mentioned had seen
5. began had done

In Your Own Words

1. First: It had begun to rain.
   Second: The fans started to leave.
   The fans started to leave after it had begun to rain.
2. First: I realized that I had been robbed.
   Second: I noticed the door was open.
   I realized that I had been robbed after I noticed that the door was open.
3. First: I had already made an improper turn.
   Second: I saw the policeman.
   I had already made an improper turn before I saw the policeman.

In Your Own Words

1. After I had changed the flat tire at 3:00, I hurried to meet you.
2. Before Frank drank the beer, he had already given me the keys.
3. Duane and I drove to the lake after we had picked up the camping gear.

LESSON 22: Future Perfect Tense

Try It Out

1. reads will have read
2. will have finished get
3. eat will have eaten
4. sees will have gotten
5. calls will have made

In Your Own Words

1. By the time you see me, I will have picked up my new car.
2. If you continue to eat like that, you will look like a blimp.
3. I will have received the check by next week.
4. Unless I get some sleep, I will feel too tired tomorrow.
5. I will become very nervous before we get there.

In Your Own Words

1. By the time I finish work, I will have missed the game.
2. By the time Harry gets his license, he will have become an old man.
3. By next New Year's Day, I will have lost 30 pounds.

Check Your Skills: Use the Present Perfect Tense

1. has grown
2. have just eaten
2. has gotten
4. has met
5. have never left
6. That plant's grown two inches since yesterday.
7. You've just eaten the last cookie.
8. The weather's gotten colder in the last few days.
9. I think she's met you before.
10. They've never left their children alone.

Check Your Skills: Use the Past Perfect Tense

1. had driven
2. had run
3. had known
4. had taken
5. had rung
6. We'd driven that car for six years before it needed any repairs.
7. After he'd run the first three miles of the race, he decided to quit.
8. They'd known about it for weeks, but they only told me about it yesterday.
9. I'd taken ten pictures before I realized that there was no film in the camera.

Check Your Skills: Use the Future Perfect Tense

1. will have beaten
2. will have eaten
3. will have begun

Check Your Skills: Write about Actions with the Perfect Tenses

1. has just worn — a
2. had never flown — b
3. have never been — b
4. will have bought — c
5. had drawn — b
6. had said — c
7. has paid — c
8. will have come — c

UNIT 4 MASTERY REVIEW

Show What You Know

If you have ever boiled water, you can make perfect hard-cooked eggs. After you have picked two or three eggs, you'll check that their shells have no cracks. You will have also already filled a saucepan with enough cold water to cover the eggs with an inch of water. You will have added a teaspoon of salt to the water, too, to help harden the shells. When everything is ready, you'll use a medium-high flame to bring the water to boil. When the water has bubbled for a minute, you'll cover the pan and turn off the heat. After the eggs have sat for fifteen to twenty minutes, you'll pour the very hot water out of the pan and run cold water over the warm eggs. And that's all there is to it! You will have made perfect hard-cooked eggs with smooth, uncracked shells. I myself had wondered for years how the trick was done, and I was amazed to learn how easy it actually was!

FINAL MASTERY TEST

1. needs
2. are
3. was
4. were
5. Are take
6. were sign
7. is talking
8. are planning
9. was getting
10. were enjoying
11. will be sleeping
12. will be watching
13. was keeping
14. will be arriving
15. has encouraged
16. might have
17. must be
18. should eat
19. do like
20. are actually selling
21. did clean
22. has driven
23. have seen
24. have watched
25. have sworn
26. had lived
27. had cleaned
28. will have left
29. will have been
30. will have painted
31. me
32. he
33. us
34. we
35. them
36. her
37. me
38. him
39. specifically
40. sweet
41. unhappy
42. tired
43. well
44. loud
45. noisily
46. quickly
47. quiet
48. awfully badly
49. really well
50. loudly